THE

REVOLUTIONARY

LEADER

What People Are Saying About

The Revolutionary Leader

This book lives up to its title! It is filled with practical, down-to-life advice for those looking forward to becoming revolutionary leaders.

RORY TATE, Senior Pastor
Center of Hope Bible Fellowship

Wow. How refreshing is *The Revolutionary Leader*, when I began to read it I wasn't able to put it down. The revelation and insight Stephen gives about leadership is on time spiritually and effective for this time in history.

Ken Johnson, Senior Pastor
Life Changers International Church

"The *Revolutionary Leader* is a remarkable book designed to transform lives. Stephen Owens writings emerge from both an ethical and theological framework which holds significant truths for those in the religious, political, social and civic arena. I am honored to recommend this book to you as it is an excellent synopsis of real life challenges, pertinent keys to success and a bounty of resources for embracing transformative leadership skills. A truly engaging book."

> Pastor Reno I Johnson,
> Voice of Deliverance
> Nassau, Bahamas;
> Author of, *Lord, Why...?*

In *The Revolutionary Leader*, Stephen Owens' interpretation of Scripture provides inspiration in developing personal leadership skills. His specific action plan will not only help you become a more effective leader, but will also help you lead a more purposeful life.

> Lori K. Long, Ph.D., Associate Professor,
> Baldwin-Wallace College,
> Author of *The Parent's Guide to Family Friendly Work*

The Revolutionary Leader is a divine inspiration that will enlighten & encourage leaders to seek Godly wisdom and guidance. It will inspire you to desire and follow the vision God has for you. It also urges you to cultivate the gifts within you to become a more effective leader. I pray that this God given wisdom and knowledge will transform the lives of all who read it.

> Pastor Michael L. Broome II
> Faith Works Community Church

THE REVOLUTIONARY LEADER

Life-changing, revelatory and empowering, Elder Stephen Owens has given us a priceless instrument that will completely shift our thinking in the Body of Christ. *The Revolutionary Leader* breaks the finite boundaries that keeps us locked into one dimensional thinking in the church and teaches us how to move from the ordinary into the extraordinary starting right now. This book is a must read, if you have Kingdom vision and know that you desire to see tangible manifestation in your life. It is up to you....YOU manifest the Kingdom of God in your life today!

Prophetess Kelly Crews
Kelly Crews Ministries

Stephen, I fully endorse your book, everyone who's striving to be a leader in the 21st century needs to read this book.

Doug Roth, Youth For
Christ-City Life
Director of Mentoring At
Risk Youth

This book reminds me of a Hallelujah Chorus; strong, skillful and reverent. It's been a long time since I've read anything quite so wonderful. It was a joyful read from beginning to end. Stephen Owens is a virtuoso because of his unerring teaching concerning the Word of God. This book speaks seriously about godly leadership in a honesty and straight to the point manner.

> Dr. Ronald N. Owens, Senior Pastor
> Greater Mount Ararat M.B.C.,
> Cleveland, Ohio

The Revolutionary Leader is a well thought out book. It is a must read for everyone who wants to see their lives transformed. This book will equip you with kingdom principles that will allow you to do kingdom business for the king Jesus Christ here on earth. Simply, it is a great book. Stephen Owens has written a master piece. A leadership book for all who are in leadership.

> Pastor Erik Howard
> The Gospel Church, Maple Heights,
> Ohio

Stephen Owens has given a new perspective to the definition of leadership. *The Revolutionary Leader* brings clarity to the body of Christ in regards to leadership. From Wall Street to Main Street, the world is void of sincere leaders who are willing to go against the staus quo in regards to proper leadership. This void is even more apparent in the Body of Christ and Stephen truly demonstrates the need and optimism of Kingdom Leadership. I highly encourage every leader to read this book and help manifest the Kingdom of God in their life.

Kent Wise, Pastor, Motivational
Speaker, Entrepreneur

In *The Revolutionary Leader* Stephen masterfully explains the steps needed to be taken to actualize a vision.

Michael Paul Valentine/ "The Plan Doctor"
Author of *The E-Pill*

This text by Stephen Owens is a visionary work that brilliantly intertwines personal growth with the power of God's spirit. A vision of incorporating the power God gives us to help create a revolution of personal potential!

Dr. Sean Gilmore, Associate Professor of
Communication
Baldwin-Wallace College

THE

REVOLUTIONARY

LEADER

Manifesting Kingdom Leadership

Stephen D. Owens

STEPHEN D. OWENS

Table of Contents

Forward

Many books have been written about "Leadership" however what makes *The Revolutionary Leader* unique and different is that *The Revolutionary Leader* is based on the teachings to the bible. The Bible teaches us that leadership is a call from God, not the opinion or call from man. Those called and prepared by God for leadership are recognized as leaders by others and proved as leaders by their character and legacy. *The Revolutionary Leader* teaches us that all of us in the body of Christ are leaders in some shape, form or fashion. Fear of failure is the one of the primary reason that stops some of us from answering the call to be a leader. You don't have to lead a large group to be leader. Leadership sometimes begins in smaller ways first and with the power of prayer.

I have had the pleasure of witnessing Stephen Owens delivering his powerful message of Leadership. Stephen brings all of his passion, knowledge and commitment to sharing the biblical principals of leadership to his audience in a most insightful and provocative way. This message is most timely and needed across the country as we face many challenges in our present time.

I am encouraged through Stephen's message about leadership as he brings to light the fundamentals of leadership that I work to exhibit in all facets of my professional and personal life. As a Councilman, a business executive at work and president of many organizations, I have found that people need the right information to help them succeed. They need a skilled leader who exhibit confidence in oneself and others, create and communicate a vision, strive for excellence, demonstrate passion and enthusiasm, treat everyone with respect and dignity and believe in the power of praying. A leader must set the example for others to follow. As such, a leader must maintain the highest standards of honesty and integrity.

I've had the opportunity to observe and learn from many leaders and found that each of them exhibit the following   traits:

1) **Have Confidence in Yourself and Others:** Most people shy away from leadership roles because they lack confidence in their own ability to be an effective leader. You cannot expect people to follow you if you don't have confidence in yourself and your team. Sometimes the tasks ahead may seem enormous and challenging but you have to look at challenges as opportunities. Confidence is about believing in yourself and your team. A leader must have and reinforce an optimistic outlook.

2) **Articulate a compelling Vision**: Leaders must create a specific, consistent and memorable vision of their goals. They must be able to articulate their vision consistently so everyone is moving in the same direction to accomplish

that goal. During my four years as President of the National Black MBA Association Cleveland/Northeast Ohio Chapter, my vision was "to receive Chapter of the Year Award each year. This vision was communicated over and over again so everyone understood what we were working towards. Short term goals was set and achieved. In the end, the Chapter won Chapter of the Award for four consecutive years. That's the power of creating a specific and memorable vision and setting short term attainable goals that need to be accomplished to make that vision become reality.

3) **Strive for Excellence:** As a leader we must go far beyond the call of duty, doing more than others expect. This is what excellence is all about. Excellence means doing your very best, in everything, in every way. Charles Kendall Adams wrote. "No one ever attains very eminent success by simply doing what is required of him; it is the amount and excellence of that is over and above the required that determines the greatness of ultimate distinction." You must set your expectation high, surround yourself with people whose integrity and values you respect, get their agreement on a course of action and give them your ultimate trust.

4) **Demonstrate Passion and Enthusiasm**: Successful leaders have an abundance of passion and enthusiasm for what they are trying

to accomplish. Passion is something that you cannot teach, you either have it or you don't. People often asked me what should they get involved with and my answer is "What are you passionate about? People tend to resist what which is forced upon them and flourish at the things they are passionate about. When you are passionate about what you do it doesn't become work and you find yourself with much more energy to accomplish your goals.

5) **Believe in the Power of Prayer**: Prayer is our way of talking to God and asking him for guidance. It our personal time with God. Matthew 14:23, it says, "And when He had sent the multitudes away, He went up into a mountain apart to pray: and when the evening was come, he was there alone." If Jesus needed to go off and pray, how much more do we need to? Praying should not be something we do out of duty and routine. Prayer is talking and listening and asking him for guidance.

Leadership is a blessing and a gift from God to move forward His people for His causes. All of us were put on earth for a purpose. It's up to us to find that purpose and transform our lives through the word of God.

Alton Tinker
Founder
Society of Urban Professionals (SOUP)

The Introduction

This book is written to my brothers and sisters in Christ who are looking for more out of life. They do not want to live life being average. I hope this book encourages and compels you to reach for your purpose and achieve the vision God has given you.

It is time for a revolution to be launched on the status quo of leadership as usual. As I write this book the words of the British statesmen Benjamin Disraeli comes to mind when he declared, "I have been ever of the opinion that revolutions are not to be evaded" (1).

I believe we are in the season where God is ready to manifest His power in the lives of ordinary saints like you and me. I am convinced that the Almighty God of heaven and earth is moving the Church back to our Biblical roots of the first century. The Holy Spirit is guiding us to focus on that which is of the utmost importance – "The Gospel of Jesus and The Kingdom of God".

It is time out for Church as usual in the twenty-first century. God is stirring up individuals who are willing to do his will so he can manifest his kingdom on earth. Manifesting a kingdom presence on earth is to do what Jesus taught in the Lord's Prayer, "Thy kingdom come Thy will be done in earth, as it is in heaven" (Matt. 6:10 KJV). Having the kingdom of God made apparent in earth is to allow the will of God to be done in our lives.

We as the church must understand that the Kingdom of God was on the forefront of the minds of the New Testament disciples. Their main concern was not, "Are we going to have red or blue carpet in the fellowship hall?" They were not overly concerned whether they would have chicken and mashed potatoes after revival or if they were going to have a roast with green beans. Their main concern was to declare the Gospel of Jesus and the Kingdom of God to a dying world. This is what this book is about: **<u>YOU</u>** manifesting the Kingdom of God in your life.

Who were some of the people in the New Testament who talked about the Kingdom of God during their ministry? If we were to start at the beginning of the New Testament with the Gospels, the first individual we would find declaring the Kingdom of God, or the Kingdom of Heaven, is John the Baptist. Matthew 3:1, 2 KJV.reads, "In those days come John the Baptist, preaching in the wilderness of Judea, and saying, Repent ye: for the kingdom of heaven is at hand."

The next person we would find would be our Savior and Lord, Jesus the Christ. We can visit Matthew's writing again and see that the Kingdom of God was a major part of his ministry and message. "From that time Jesus began to preach, and to say, Repent: for the kingdom of heaven is at hand" (Matt. 4:17 KJV).

The last person we will look at is the Apostle Paul. The Kingdom of God was extremely important to his ministry. Doctor Luke, the beloved physician, recorded in the close of his second letter to Theophilus, which is known as the Acts of the Apostles, that Paul focused on preaching the Kingdom of God. "Then Paul dwelt two whole years in his own rented house, and received all who came to him, preaching the kingdom of God and teaching the things which concern the Lord Jesus Christ with all confidence, no one forbidding him" (Acts 2:30,31 NKJV New King James Version).

The Kingdom of God focuses on the rule, regency, and authority of God. Wherever the Kingdom of God is made apparent, God's rule and control is shown. Whenever we read that the Kingdom of God is at hand, God's regency is present. That means his ambassadors are declaring the sovereign governmental order of the Almighty King of Glory.

Whenever God is manifesting his authority, the power of his kingdom is being displayed. The Kingdom of God is being manifested on the earth in its spiritual form during this dispensation, but there will come a day when the kingdoms of the earth will come under the sovereign control of the Kingdom of Heaven.

The Kingdom of God must not be forgotten in the twenty-first century church. No longer can we allow denominations and man-made traditions to divide the body of Christ. Focusing only on denominations will breed division in the body. The Kingdom of God produces unity and oneness.

Concentrating on man-made traditions and ordinances will breed bondage to rules and laws. The Kingdom of God produces liberty and freedom to do God's will for your life. When the Kingdom of God is manifested in the life of a believer, a whole new world of possibilities – a world full of potential, hope, and reconciliation – opens.

Let us look at Jesus and see the Kingdom of God being displayed in his life and ministry. Jesus is the perfect example of a kingdom ambassador manifesting the Kingdom of God through his lifestyle. Let us read a few passages from the Gospel of Matthew 11:2 – 5 KJV.

Now when John had heard in the prison the works of Christ, he sent two of his disciples, and said unto him, Art thou he that should come, or do we look for another? Jesus answered and said unto them, Go and shew John again those things which ye do hear and see: the blind receive their sight, and the lame walk, the lepers are cleaned, and the deaf hear, the dead is raised up, and the poor have the gospel preached to them.

The Bible tells us that John sent two of his disciples to question Jesus to find out if he was the Messiah. Jesus told them to go and tell John what they had heard and seen. Blind people can now see. Lame folks can now walk. Incurable diseases (leprosy) have been removed from individuals.

People who were deaf can now hear. People who were dead are now alive. We cannot forget that the poor have heard the gospel, so now they have a future to look forward to. The information that Jesus told John's disciples is what the Kingdom of God is all about. The Kingdom is about transforming lives so that they can be filled with possibility and hope.

This is what this book is all about – **transforming lives**. Helping my Christian family to see that there is a world of possibilities open to you, because you are a part of the family and Kingdom of God. The Bible tells us in John 1:12 that once we believe in the gospel of Jesus we are endowed with the power to become the sons of God.

That's correct, Women, you too are considered a son of the Most High God. The Apostle Paul tells us in Galatians 3:28 KJV, "There is neither Jew nor Greek, there is neither bond nor free, there is neither male nor female: for ye are all one in Christ Jesus."

When we become a part of the family of God, we are restored to our rightful place as being kings and priests unto God. Revelations 1:16 declares, "And hath made us kings and priests unto God and his Father, to him be glory and dominion for ever and ever, Amen." Based on that verse, we can say that the Kingdom of God is full of kings and priests.

This is why the Apostle Peter says in 1 Peter 2:9 KJV, "But ye are a chosen generation, a royal priesthood, a holy nation, a peculiar people; that ye should shew forth the praise of him who hath called you out of darkness into his marvellous light".

The Kingdom of God is really a kingdom of kings manifesting the will of the KING on the earth. Now, a king is the same thing as a leader. Since we are kings, not the KING, in the Kingdom of God, we are positioned to become leaders.

Understand then, that because you are a king, you are a leader. The information compiled in this book is to help you develop your leadership. Since God is our Father, we should do his will for our lives and be successful while doing it. Now, we are not talking about what the world calls success.

* Money   *Prestige
*Recognition   *Big house
*Power   *Expensive toys
*Influence   *Lavish lifestyle

All of those things are nice to have when they are put into their proper place. It's okay to have money, a big house, and expensive toys as long as you are in control of them, and they are not in control of you.

This topic brings to mind what Dr. Bill Hamon wrote in his book *The Day of the Saints*. He declared, "Success according to God's standard is not based upon the world's ideas of success, but upon whether a person is fulfilling his calling and ministry regardless of what or where it is" (2). Succeeding at being a leader is not about having a lot of stuff. It is about fulfilling the will of God for your life.

This book is entitled *The Revolutionary Leader* because Christians must transform the role of leadership by doing the will of God. This book is an attempt to equip you to do the work of the ministry, as Ephesians 4:11-12 KJV declares: "And he gave some apostles; and some, prophets; and some, evangelists; and some, pastors and teachers; for the perfecting of the saints, for the work of the ministry, for the edifying of the body of Christ."

The concept of the average Christian being a leader is radical to many believers. Many Christians understand when we say that pastors, bishops, politicians, chief executive officers, and people with those types of titles are leaders. Yet many of us don't understand that every one of us in the body of Christ is a leader in some shape, form, or fashion.

As you journey through this book, my prayer and hope is that God ignites a fire in your inner man to want to do the will of God. I hope that a new world filled with possibilities opens up to you, and you start to see that God has a plan and a purpose for your life.

*

A Vision is a bull's eye – the target you are shooting for in the future.

Your Vision is a major goal that God wants you to accomplish.

*

Chapter One:
A Revealed Vision

Where there is no vision the people perish.
                                    -Proverbs 29:18-

All Christians are leaders. It does not matter how many people you are leading. It doesn't even matter if you have no one following you. That does not negate who you were created to be - - A LEADER!

Leadership deals with Mobilization, Energizing, and Encouraging. We have to mobilize people. We have to work to create positive energy within our teams as well as encourage them to succeed. You may say, "I do not have anyone following me." That's okay.

That just means you have to start mobilizing, energizing and encouraging yourself. These three functions of leadership must be done if you're leading thousands or you are dealing with personal leadership. You will learn more about this in Chapter Five.

Who are leaders in the Christian community?
  1. Parents – They lead their families.
  2. Pastors – They lead a congregation.
  3. Legislators – They lead states.
  4. Executives – They lead companies.

5. Individuals – They lead themselves and other to be more like Christ.

As believers, we must work on ourselves before we can work on others. Jesus declared in Matthew 7:5 KJV, "Thou hypocrites, first cast out the beam out of thine own eye; and then shalt thou see clearly to cast out the mote out of thy brother's eye." In essence, what He is saying is to work on yourself before you try to work on others.

Leadership always starts individually then moves out collectively. You must lead yourself before you can lead others. You cannot direct another person's actions if you cannot direct your own.

Now this aspect of leading your life deals with you, directing your life to fall in line with the leadership and guidance of the Holy Ghost. John 16:13 NLT (New Living Translation) declares, "When the Spirit of truth comes, he will guide you into all truth. He will not be presenting his own ideas: he will be telling you what he has heard. He will tell you about the future."

In this verse the Spirit of truth, which is the Holy Spirit, will guide us. Jesus did not say that the Holy Spirit would make us follow him. This scripture is showing us that we have to decide to follow the Spirit of truth.

Vision

A great place to begin the conversation about leadership is with vision. A vision is something to strive for and to shoot at. It is something you reach for. We all need a target, a bull's eye, to direct our energy towards.

That vision may be to plant a church, to reach a community or a demographic, to start or buy a business. God may show you he wants you to have a harmonious household, or to be a loving and caring spouse, or to be an encouraging and supportive parent. God may lead you to go into the political area.

Whatever the vision is, it should not be something you create. Your vision should be something that has been revealed from God. Your vision should be based on a revelation from God. Henry Blackaby tells us in his book *Chosen to be God's Prophet*:

> Many in our day do not operate by revelation but vision. Because many have so adapted to the world, they have let the world's method of leadership control them. The world's thinking says that you cannot be a leader unless you have a vision. However, the people of God are not to be a people of vision; they are to be a people of revelation.

It should be something that God has uncovered for you to pursue and not made up in your spare time.

Now when I say the vision should be a revelation from God, I am not saying that what God show us will be equal to his complete inspired and infallible revelation, the Bible.

The revelation I am writing about is when God leads you to go after a specific goal. God must inspire our visions; they must not be something that came from our imaginations. The word of God declares that, what seems right to man is evil in the eyes of our God.

Your vision is a part of the will of God for your life. Your vision is a major accomplishment that God wants you to achieve for His glory. **This is one of your assignments from Heaven.**

The Bible tells us that without a vision people will die a slow death. Their lives will wither and go into a state of atrophy and die, because they are not being used to their fullest potential.

Proverbs 29:18 KJV proclaims, "Where there is no vision the people perish." The wisest man to live, besides Jesus Christ, spoke this proverb. That man was King Solomon, the third king of the nation of Israel. There are two words that need to be explained from this proverb, and they are *vision* and *perish*. These words can be translated in a few different words in Hebrew.

1. Vision – sight, dream, revelation, and oracle (1).

29

2. Perish – loosen, expose, dismiss, absolve, and begin (2).

Let us use a couple of these words to help us understand what King Solomon was saying to us.

*Where there is *no revelation* the people will be dismissed.
*Where there is *no sight* the people will be loosed.

A leader's vision must be based on God's revelation so her followers will not be dismissed and scattered abroad. A leader's vision produces sight into the future to keep her and her troops focused and working together as a team. The leader's vision should be a compelling dream that was produced from a revelation given by God.

This dream will captivate people so they will stay fixed on the goals for the future. The leader must also be the oracle for the vision, declaring to the people that there is somewhere we have to strive towards. Being a proclaimer of possibility will stop your family, your business, your fellowship, and your nation from repeating a cycle of being average.

Many people are average because they start something, then stop, and they never complete anything. The more we proclaim a better future for the multitude; the more people will accomplish things, because we as leaders are helping them to stay focused. We must understand that vision produces forward momentum.

The Way God Speaks

There are a number of ways God can uncover a revelation.

1. **The Bible** – Written, complete, inspired, and infallible word of God.
2. **The voice of God** – God uses the Holy Spirit to speak to us.
3. **Dreams** – being asleep
4. **Vision** – day-dreaming while being awake
5. **Prophetic utterance** – someone speaking a word from the Lord
6. **Circumstance** – by your environment and the things you go through

Here are a few examples from Scripture to solidify what is being expressed here.

The Bible

The first place we must begin as we talk about the way God speaks is with the Bible. The Bible is the inspired, inerrant, and infallible word of God. As a follower of Jesus, the standard for our lives is Jesus and the Bible. The Bible tells us how Jesus lived and how we are supposed to live. The Bible tells us in 2 Timothy 3:16 - 17 NLT:

All Scripture is inspired by God and is useful to teach us what is true and to make us realize what is wrong in our lives. It straightens us out and teaches us to do what is right.

It is God's way of preparing us in every way, fully equipped for every good thing God wants us to do.

This means that the very words of the Bible came from God. The Bible's purpose is to:

- Teach us the truth about life.
- Show what we are doing wrong.
- Teach us the right way to live.
- Prepare and equip us to do everything God wants us to do.

When you are trying to find out what God wants you to do in life, the first place you must go is to the Bible. Then when God shows you the vision, make sure it lines up with the Bible. If the vision goes against the Bible, it is not from God. The Bible will also show you how to behave when God will give you the vision. Do not overlook the Bible. It is our first and final resource on earth.

The voice of God

God uses His Holy Spirit to speak to us and to direct our lives.

Howbeit when he, the Spirit of truth, is come, he will guide you into all truth: for he shall not speak of himself; but whatsoever he shall hear, that shall he speak: and he will shew you things to come.

He shall glorify me: for he shall receive of mine, and shall shew it unto you. All things that the Father hath are mine: therefore said I, that he shall take of mine, and shall shew it unto you. (John 16:13-15)

The Holy Spirit is the Spirit of truth. He is also the Third Person within the Godhead, who dwells within all born-again believers. Ephesians 1:13, 14 NLT says,

And now you also have heard the truth, the good news that God saves you. And when you believed in Christ, he identified you as his own by giving you the Holy Spirit, whom he promised long ago.

The Spirit is God's guarantee that he will give us everything he promised and that he has purchased us to be his own people. This is just one more reason for us to praise our glorious God.

Within the few passages of John chapter 16, we are exposed to some of the activities of the Holy Spirit's ministry to the believer. The Bible tells us that he will guide us into all truth. It also declares that he shall speak to us the things that he has heard.

Jesus says that the information the Holy Spirit shall speak is not to glorify himself but to glorify Jesus. We are also told that He will shew us things to come. The word *shew* means to announce in detail (4).

One of the things the Spirit will announce to us, the Church, is what will happen in the future. This is exactly what the Holy Spirit did in Acts 11:27-30, through the Prophet Agabus. The Holy Spirit announced to the Church that there was going to be a great famine, which "came to pass in the days of Claudius Caesar" (Acts 11:28).

The Holy Spirit want to lead us and show us what God has for us in the future.

Dreams

God spoke to Joseph, the husband of the Virgin Mary, through a dream.

> And when they were departed, behold, the angel of the Lord appeareth to Joseph in a dream, saying, Arise, and take the young child and his mother, and flee into Egypt, and be thou there until I bring thee word: for Herod will seek the young child to destroy him.

> When he arose, he took the young child and his mother by night, and departed into Egypt: And was there until the death of Herod: that it might be fulfilled which was spoken of the Lord by

the prophet, saying, Out of Egypt have I called my son. (Matt. 2:13-15)

The angel of the Lord appeared to Joseph in a dream to warn him of the danger that would befall Jesus if they stayed where they were. The angel also gave him directions as to where to take Mary and baby Jesus. One of the functions of angels is to be a messenger for the Most High God. Therefore, when the angel is speaking he is communicating the words of God. Here is another example from the life of Joseph.

But when Herod was dead, behold an angel of the Lord appeareth in a dream to Joseph in Egypt, Saying, Arise, and take the young child and his mother, and go into the land of Israel: for they are dead which sought the young child's life. And he arose, and took the young child and his mother, and came into the land of Israel.

But when he heard that Archelaus did reign in Judea in the room of his father Herod, he was afraid to go thither: notwithstanding, being warned of God in a dream, he turned aside into the parts of Galilee: and he came and dwelt in a city called Nazareth: that it might be fulfilled which was spoken by the prophets, He shall be called a Nazarene. (Matt. 2:19-23)

Two dreams have occurred within these verses. In verse nineteen, this is the first dream. The angel of the Lord appeared to Joseph again, but this time the angel gave him direction to leave the land of Egypt and go into the land of Israel.

While on his way to the land of Israel, God warned him in another dream concerning what was going on in Judea. Joseph was informed that Herod's son Archelaus had taken control in Judea. Joseph was afraid, and went to live in Galilee with Mary and baby Jesus.

The Lord used an angel in a dream to tell Joseph information. God may not necessarily use an angel in a dream to tell you his vision for you. The objective is not to look for angels, but to look to God to tell you want he wants done.

Visions

Ananias had a vision; and our Lord Jesus was talking to him about Saul, of Tarsus. Most people know him as the Apostle Paul.

> "And there was a certain disciple at Damascus, named Ananias; and to him said the Lord in a vision, Ananias. And he said, Behold I am here, Lord. And the Lord said unto him, Arise, and go into the street which is called Straight, and enquire in the house of Judas for one called Saul, of Tarsus: for, behold, he prayeth, and hath seen in a vision a man named Ananias coming in, and putting his hand on him, that he might receive his sight. (Acts 9:10-12)

36

The Lord directed Ananias through a vision to go to a specific place, "the house of Judas", and to meet a specific person, Saul. A vision from this text is basically a daydream. I believe God can still be that clear with us today. We must continually seek him in prayer to find out what he will have us do with our lives.

Prophetic utterance

A Prophet from Jerusalem by the name of Agabus was at the city of Antioch and prophesied that there was going to be a great famine in the land.

> And in the days came prophets from Jerusalem unto Antioch. And there stood up one of them named Agabus, and signified by the Spirit that there should be a great dearth throughout all the world: which came to pass in the days of Claudius Caesar. Then the disciples, every man according to his ability, determined to send relief unto the brethren which dwelt in Judea: Which also they did, and sent it to the elders by the hands of Barnabas and Saul. (Acts 11:27-30)

From these verses, the first fact that must be pointed out is that God speaks through a person. The New Testament Prophets communicated the word of the Lord to people of the Lord. In verse twenty-seven it said, "prophets from Jerusalem" came to Antioch. There were a group of them who came from Jerusalem.

The second truth is found in verse 28, and it declares that the prophet Agabus stood up and *"signified by the Spirit"* that there was going to be a famine. The word *signified* means to indicate (3). He pointed out to the brethren at Antioch what was about to happen on the earth. Based on that prophetic word, the disciples in Antioch raised money to help those in need and sent the money to Judea.

God showed the Antioch church what was about to happen through the encouraging words of Agabus. The church at Antioch was inspired (got a vision) to help the Jerusalem church. We must have people in the church who are not afraid to tell us what they believe God has said.

Remember, what they say is not infallible like the Bible, yet it may be something that God wants us to help with. We must check what they say in light of what the Bible says. The Bible is the final authority.

Circumstance

The disciples of the first century church spread the Gospel of Jesus because of persecution.

> And Saul was consenting unto his death. And at that time there was a great persecution against the church, which was at Jerusalem; and they were all scattered abroad throughout the regions of Judea and Samaria, except the apostles.

And devout men carried Stephen to his burial, and made great lamentation over him. As for Saul, he made havoc of the church, entering into every house, and haling men and women committed them to prison. Therefore they that were scattered abroad went every where preaching the word. (Acts 8:1-4)

During this time in church history, the disciples were comfortable within the confines of Jerusalem. The message concerning the Lord Jesus Christ (the Gospel) and the Kingdom of God was not being preached throughout the known world.

When the environment in Jerusalem became hostile towards the Christian community, the believers in that location left so they would not be persecuted. The early church's mission of preaching the gospel was produced by their circumstances -- the persecution which they encountered in their city.

There may be times in life when God is ready for you to do something different, so he will allow you to enter into difficult situations. Those circumstances are to draw you to him for direction and to move you towards the tasks he wants you to accomplish.

It is God's prerogative to uses a dream to reveal to you your vision, or if he chooses someone to prophecy into your life. The main concern is to make sure that it is from God. This will require you to study the Bible, to pray fervently, and to get wise and godly counsel.

STEPHEN D. OWENS

Hearing the Shepherd's voice

We must be able to hear and recognize the voice of God. This is of crucial importance if you desire to fulfill the will of God. Jesus said in John 10:2-4, 14:

> But he that entereth in by the door is the shepherd of the sheep. To him the porter openeth; and the sheep hear his voice: and he calleth his own sheep by name, and leadeth them out. And when he putteth forth his own sheep, he goeth before them, and the sheep follow him: for they know his voice. I am the good Shepherd, and know my sheep, and am known of mine.

In these verses, Jesus is telling us about the relationship of a shepherd and his sheep. He says that a shepherd speaks to his sheep. He knows his sheep by name.

Jesus said that when a shepherd sends out his sheep, he is in front of them, guiding them. Jesus declares that the sheep hear and know the voice of their shepherd. In verse 14, Jesus proclaims that he is the good shepherd and he knows his sheep (followers) and his sheep (followers) know him.

The followers of Christ are his disciples, and his disciples listen when he speaks to them because they know he talking. As followers of Jesus Christ we must know his voice.

40

Let us examine two words and their meanings from John 10:4, 14:

1. Know – To see (5).
2. Voice_ – Disclosure, a tone, address, saying, language (6).

As we look at these two words, we will get a better understanding of what it means to know the voice of God. The word *know* in the Greek means "to see." The implication is to know the voice of God by being able to see God.

We have to be able to see the way God speaks to His people. We **must** be able to see and observe the ways of God. Christians have the ability to see the ways of God because He has given us sight, so that we will be able to see and comprehend His activity. Those that are not blood-washed believers are blind to the things of God.

The Bible tells us in 2 Corinthians 4:4, "In whom the god of this world hath blinded the minds of them which believe not, lest the light of the glorious gospel of Christ, who is the image of God, should shine unto them."

The word *voice* in the Greek has a few different meanings, but they all can be used to get a better understanding of the way God speaks.

• You must be able to see how God discloses His messages.

41

- You need to be able to know the <u>tone</u> of God when He is pleased, when He is happy, and when He is angry and grieved.

- You must know through observation how God <u>addresses</u> issues and problems.

- You have to know the <u>sayings</u> of God by reading and studying the Bible.

- You need to know the <u>language</u> of God when He is speaking in your prayer time, in your dreams, in a vision, and through prophetic people.

When we get a better understanding of these concepts, we will be able to know when the Lord is speaking to us. We want to cultivate our ear to the voice of God so that we will be able to respond when he is telling us to do something. We must understand that when God reveal something to us, that information will never contradict the Bible.

Every idea, every vision, and every word you believe God has given you must line up with scripture. This is a very important point to understand: all visions from God will be confirmed by His complete, inspired, and infallible written Word, the Bible.

Spiritual Discernment

When God reveals to you your vision he may allow you to spiritually discern it; some of our brothers in the East would call this intuition. This is when God allows you to sense something in your spirit.

Watchman Nee phrases it like this: " This spiritual sensing is called intuition, for it impinges directly without reason or cause. Without passing through any procedure, it comes forth in a straight manner... Spiritual sense... does not require any outside cause but emerges directly from within" (7).

Spiritual discernment is a function of our spirit. Spiritual discernment gives us the ability to "know" something. You may not be able to explain it, but you "know" that something is going to happen. You might not understand it, but you "know" that this is what you are supposed to do.

Spiritual discernment is when you "know" something beyond a shadow of a doubt. Dr. Tony Evan, in his book *Kingdom Agenda,* declared, "We can know intuitively, despite circumstances, that God is in control, working things together that look out of control." (8)

It is recorded in the Gospel of Mark and in the Book of Acts that Jesus and the Apostle Paul both used spiritual discernment. The Gospel of Mark declares, "And immediately when Jesus perceived in his spirit that they so reasoned within themselves, he said unto

43

them, Why reason ye these things in your heart?"
(Mark 2:8)

The scripture declared, "Jesus perceived in his
spirit" the thoughts of the scribes in Mark 2:6. The
word *perceived* means to know upon, recognize, to
become fully acquainted with (9). Therefore, Jesus
recognized and became fully acquainted with the
thought of the scribes within his spirit. He knew what
they were thinking within his spirit. He spiritually
discerned their thoughts. While we will not be able to
know the thoughts of people like Jesus, that does not
mean we cannot have spiritual·discernment.

All we have to do is refer to the Apostle Paul.
Luke wrote in the book of Acts, "The same heard Paul
speak: who steadfastly beholding him, and perceiving
that he had faith to be healed" (Acts 14:9). We see in
this verse that the Apostle Paul perceived that the
crippled man from the city of Lystra had enough faith
to be healed.

In this verse, the translators used the same word
but in a different tense to show that Paul was operating
in spiritual discernment, just like Jesus was in Mark
2:8. Paul was able to see that this man had the faith to
walk, because he knew in his spirit what was
happening inside of the crippled man. The Holy Spirit
revealed to Paul that this crippled man had enough
faith to be healed.

Plan of Action

To reach your vision, seek God diligently in order for him to counsel you in creating a plan of action so you can accomplish it. Your plan of action will be a list of tasks to complete within a specific timeframe. The plan will be a set of goals that need to be accomplished before you arrive at your vision.

You must connect your vision, your major goal, to smaller goals. What you are doing is building upon achievements to help motivate yourself to be persistent in achieving the vision. We must make sure we write our goals and vision on paper. Stephen R. Covey wrote, "writing is a psycho-neuromuscular activity and literally imprints the brain" (10).

The book of Proverbs gives us encouragement to make sure we have goals in life. Proverbs 11:27 NLT declares, "If your goals are good, you will be respected." People will respect you when your goals are solid and filled with goodness.

Goals needed to accomplish your vision:

1. Immediate Goals – Tasks you can do right now
2. Intermediate Goals – These are milestones, the objectives that must be accomplished in one month, six months, and one year.
3. Long-term Goals – The manifestation of the vision in two years, five years or ten years.

Your goal-setting process is crucial to manifesting the vision. Set aside some quiet time to talk to God. Withdraw yourself from people to meditate on the information that God has spoken to you concerning your vision.

Even Jesus had to take time to go and talk to God the Father alone. The Book of Matthew tells us this: "And when he had sent the multitude away, he went up into a mountain apart to pray: and when the evening was come, he was there alone" (Matt 14:23).

Your time line must be arranged in an orderly fashion as a *plan of execution.* You must also remember when you are setting your goals to stay flexible ,because these goals are not set in stone. Anything can happen which can throw the plan off.

The plan is to keep on track, not to beat yourself up when you don't meet your objectives in the allotted time. Your goals are targets to aim for to help bring the vision to pass. Your goals will be benchmarks on the road to completing your vision.

What we must do is research the vision God has giving us. How does it work? What does it take to build it? What does it take to operate it? What does it take to make it successful? You also must research and study people who have accomplished the same vision.

If God has you blazing a new path, study people who are pioneers, people who have lived for the glory of the Father. A great pioneer to study is our Lord and Savior Jesus the Christ.

What should we look at when we are examining the lives of pioneers?

1. How long did it take them to arrive at the vision?
2. What did they do to get to the vision?
3. What type of background and education did they have?
4. Who did they associate with?

We will use these individuals as examples, so that when times become difficult and we want to quit we will not give up. You want to be able to remember their hard times when you get discouraged. When those moments occur you will be able to tell yourself, "If they went through what they went through and accomplished their vision, so can I".

We must understand that goals and achievements vary between people. People are not the same and will not act exactly the same way. Do not get frustrated because you did not arrive at your vision at the same time as someone else. Use their experiences as benchmarks for your projections. Remember to stay prayerful while you are creating your plan of action, because God knows how long it will take you to arrive at the vision.

Abram the Visionary

Now let us turn our attention to Abram, one of the patriarchs of Israel. Abram is an example of a visionary. The Bible tells us how he received his vision.

> And the Lord said unto Abram, after that Lot was separated from him, Lift up now thine eyes, and look from the place where thou art northward, and southward, and eastward, and westward: for all the land which thou seest, to thee will I give it, and to thy seed for ever.
>
> And I will make thy seed as the dust of the earth: so that if a man can number the dust of the earth, then shall thy seed be numbered. Arise, walk through the land in the length of it and in the breadth of it; for I will give it unto thee." (Gen.13: 14-17)

This discourse was a conversation between God and Abram, whose name was changed to Abraham. God revealed to Abram that the land he was standing on was for him and his descendants. It was not a vision that he made up so he could conquer that land.

Abram knew the Lord was speaking to him because he knew the voice of the Lord. God revealed to him the land of Canaan. This was something that God wanted to bless Abram with. Abram's vision came from God.

**Once your vision has been completed,
seek God for a new one.**

Transitioning to a New Vision

To have an example of this, let us turn our attention to Joshua and the children of Israel. We have to realize that once we have accomplished one vision, we cannot stop and think we have arrived. God will give you a new vision when the previous one is completed.

When God reveals to you the next vision, don't lock God in a box by saying, "God manifested the vision like this the last time, so he is going to bring to pass the new vision the same way." That way of thinking can move you away from following God.

Yes, we understand that God does have laws and that he does move within patterns. That is why we can stand on the promises of God, because He is a God of principle and he works in seasons and cycles. But get something very clear: God's cycles and patterns are not always easily detected. We don't think the way God thinks.

God has manifold wisdom and he is all knowing, so we should not say he always works a certain way. The Bible tells us in the book of Isaiah, "For my thoughts are not your thoughts, neither are your ways my ways, saith the Lord. For as the heavens are higher than the earth, so are my ways higher than your ways, and my thoughts than your thoughts" (Isa. 55:8, 9).

Let us look at the Book of Joshua for a moment. In Joshua 6, God informed Joshua how the nation of Israel was going to capture the city of Jericho. In the first five verses of Chapter 6, God tells Joshua the strategy he has to implement in order for him to take the city. Joshua 6:1-5 declares:

> Now Jericho was straitly shut up because of the children of Israel: none went out, and none came in. And the Lord said unto Joshua, See, I have given into thine hand Jericho, and the king thereof, and the mighty men of valour. And ye shall compass the city, all ye men of war, and go round about the city once. Thus shalt thou do six days.
>
> And seven priests shall bear before the ark seven trumpets of rams' horns: and the seventh day ye shall compass the city seven times, and the priests shall blow with the trumpets. And it shall come to pass, that when they make a long blast with the ram's horn, and when ye hear the sound of the trumpet, all the people shall shout; and the wall of the city shall fall down flat, and the people shall ascend up every man straight before him.

Now let us explain these passages of scripture. The vision Joshua received from God was to take control of the city of Jericho. The Bible tells us that the city of Jericho was locked up tight and no one was coming in and no one was going out. In your own circumstances, understand there may be a time when God gives you a vision and the people who are already in that place may try to shut you out.

Even though the city was locked, God declared to Joshua that the city was his for the taking. These were the directions: for six days straight, seven priest carrying rams' horns, which are the trumpets, shall walk in front of the ark of the covenant and the men of war (soldiers) were behind the ark while they circle the city of Jericho one time.

Then on the seventh day, they were supposed to circle the city seven times. On the seventh circle the priests were suppose to blow their trumpets and when the people heard the rams' horns they were going to shout. When the soldiers let out the shout, the walls of the city were supposed to come down.

Let us look at verses 16 and 20 to see what happened when the children of Israel obeyed the plan of God.

> And it came to pass at the seventh time, when the priests blew with the trumpets, Joshua said unto the people, Shout, for the Lord hath given you the city. So the people shouted when the priests blew with the trumpets: and it came to pass, when the people heard the sound of the trumpet, and the people shouted with a great shout, that the wall fell down flat, so that the

people went up into the city, every man straight before him, and they took the city.

When they followed the directions of God, they took over the city and Joshua's vision was manifested.

The next vision God revealed to Joshua was to capture the city of Ai. Likewise, we must realize that the territories (visions) the Lord is sending us into are already occupied by someone. We will have to fight to reach our vision.

Yet, in our fight we do not use conventional weaponry. Second Corinthians 10:4 declares, "The weapons we fight with are not the weapons of the world. On the contrary, they have divine power to demolish strongholds." Let us now look at the direction God gave to Joshua concerning his vision with the city of Ai in Chapter 8 verses 1 and 2:

> And the Lord said unto Joshua, Fear not, neither be thou dismayed: take all the people of war with thee, and arise, go up to Ai: see, I have given into thy hand the king of Ai, and his people, and his city, and his land: And thou shalt do to Ai and her king as thou didst unto Jericho and her king: only the spoil thereof, and the cattle thereof, shall ye take for a prey unto yourselves: lay thee an ambush for the city behind it.

These directions were different from the directions the Lord gave to Joshua concerning the city of Jericho. There they circled the city, blew the horns and shouted, then the walls came down. With the city of Ai, God told Joshua to set up an ambush and to attack them from behind.

Joshua commanded some of his soldiers to go behind the city and wait for his command, then take the city. He then told the rest of his soldiers that they were going to confront Ai head-on, and when the men of Ai came out to fight, Israel was going to run away as if they were afraid and the men of Ai were going to follow them. The Bible tells us in verse 18 and 19:

> And the Lord said unto Joshua, Stretch out the spear that is in thy hand toward Ai; for I will give it into thine hand. And Joshua stretched out the spear that he had in his hand toward the city. And the ambush arose quickly out of their place, and they ran as soon as he had stretched out his hand; and they entered into the city, and took it, and hasted and set the city on fire.

What would have happened if Joshua would have been stuck in the mindset of, "God won the victory last time a certain way, so God will give us the victory this time the same way"? They would have lost the battle and many soldiers of the nation of Israel would have died. The point of this information is to remind us not to put God in a box. We must move as he moves and follow his directions as he gives them.

The vision that God reveals to you is a key to you discovering your reason for being alive – Your Purpose. Your visions are connected to your purpose.

Principles

1. All Christians are leaders.

2. Leadership starts individually, then moves out collectively.

3. Leadership starts with a vision.

4. Vision must be based on a revelation from God.

5. Proverbs 29:18 "Where there is no vision the people perish"

6. Every idea, every vision, and every word you believe God has given you must line up with the Bible.

7. God may allow us to use spiritual discernment in revealing to us our vision.

8. People will respect you when your goals are solid and filled with goodness.

9. Your vision is a major goal that God wants you to accomplish for His Glory.

10. Remember to connect your vision to goals.

*

Your purpose is God's will for your life.

Your purpose must be uncovered by God and not created by man.

*

STEPHEN D. OWENS

Chapter Two:
An Uncovered Purpose

*For even the Son of man came not to be minister unto,
but to minister, and to give his life as a ransom for
many.*
-Mark 10:45-

"Because the human being is created in the image of God, the will to dignity is the irreducible, psychological, spiritual nucleus around which the life of the human soul revolves and evolves. The need for dignity, self-worth, self-respect, and self-esteem is the deepest of all human needs" (1). Robert H. Schuller penned these words in his book *Self Esteem The New Reformation.*

His words shed light on why it is so important for individuals to know their purpose. Once people understand why they were created, they receive a new perspective on their lives. Knowing your purpose is the foundation upon which you are able to have a proper understanding of dignity, self-worth, self-respect, and self-esteem.

Some people think when the word *self* is used that God is left out of the picture. But as I read the scripture, I believe God wants us to know what we are worth, especially to him. He wants us to respect the bodies he gave us and to have a healthy sense of

56

appreciation about ourselves. We just need to have those areas rooted in Jesus and in what he did for us in his completed work on the cross.

A few of the most asked questions throughout the centuries are: What is the purpose of man? Why has this race been created? What is the reason behind our existence? These questions have been presented to philosophers, religious leaders, historians, and to a multitude of other people.

These questions have continued throughout generations because people are looking for meaning. They're looking for significance. We want to know we have a part to play in life. Even King David asked God, "What is man, that thou art mindful of him? And the son of man, that thou visitest him?" (Ps. 8:4)

What is meant when someone talks about having purpose? Your purpose is your reason for being alive. It's why you have been created to live here on planet Earth. It is the reason behind you being born in this time, place, century, country, province, city, family, economic situation, and the like. It is the reason and the why behind your existence.

Your purpose for being alive is what makes you unique. It is what sets you apart from the crowd. Dr. Mike Murdock, in his book *101 Wisdom Keys* declared, "Your significance is not in your similarity to another, but in your point of difference from another" (2). Stop trying to be a carbon copy of someone else.

Be yourself and let God mold you into the vessel of honor you were destined to be.

Knowing your purpose is fundamental in accomplishing your vision from God. Your purpose is God's will for your life. It is the foundational reason for you being alive. Your purpose is what God wants you to do in the totality of your life.

We play many roles in life; spouse, friend, son, daughter, employee, boss, and many more. God desires to be a part of every one of them. He wants to show you what he wants you to do in each area of your life. God's will for your life is not limited to your calling, your ministry within your local fellowship, or one particular position you hold. His will for your life encompasses your entire being.

Servant-hood

When you are operating in the will of God, you are walking in servant-hood. Jesus gives us some insight in knowing how to be good servants with the visions God has chosen us to complete.

> And that servant, which knew his lord's will, and prepared not himself, neither did according to his will, shall be beaten with many stripes. But he that knew not, and did commit things worthy of stripes, shall be beaten with few stripes. For unto whomsoever much is given, of him shall be much required: and to whom man

have committed much, of him they will ask the more." (Luke 12:47-48)

Within these two verses the Lord gives us examples of two servants. In verse 47 this servant knew his lord's will but did not do it. In verse 48 this servant did not know his lord's will so he could not accomplish it. There is something very interesting about these two servants, and it is that both servants were punished.

Understand, when you know God's will for your life, and you neither prepare yourself for it nor accomplish it, you will be whipped with many stripes. For those who know what God has called you to do, this is a very sober statement -- but it is true. Those Christians who don't know the will of God for their lives, or their purposes, are not excused from punishment either.

God's will for your life must be accomplished, and it is your responsibility to fulfill it. No more complaining that you don't know what God wants you to do. Get a firm grip on this statement: it is your responsibility to seek God diligently so he can reveal to you your reason for being alive. Jesus tells us that those individuals who do not know the Lord's will for their lives will be whipped also, but fewer times. Make sure you find out what God's will is for your life.

Vision exposes Purpose

Each vision God reveals to you exposes more of your purpose for being alive. Each vision that is manifested moves you closer to realizing your purpose. Each completed vision moves you forward to discovering all God wants you to do on this side of eternity.

When God exposes to you a glimpse of your purpose, he is giving you marching orders. The *Purpose Driven Church* by Rick Warren states, "A clear purpose not only defines what we do, it defines what we do not do" (3). When he gives you a vision, that vision is one of many visions he will give you along your walk with him.

Each vision is a major goal he wants you to achieve and each vision is a part of your overall mission in life. Your mission is to reach your destiny before you die. Your destiny is to manifest your purpose.

Dr. Henry Blackaby declared, "Further, if God has proceeded to select you for an important assignment among his people, He will thoroughly equip you with His Spirit to do it, and you will be fully accountable to obey Him, and let Him do His will through you" (4).

Life is a mission to be accomplished. It is a journey that must be completed. What is a mission? It is an assignment that a person is sent to accomplish.

Your mission is to share the Gospel of Jesus and to complete God's will for your life. A journey is when someone is traveling and progressing from one stage to another stage. We are progressing through life, traveling from one stage of life to the next stage of life.

The Bible says in 2 Corinthians 3:18, "But we all, with open face beholding as in a glass the glory of the Lord, are changed into the same image from glory to glory, even by the Spirit of the Lord."

To fulfill our purpose is a life-long pursuit.

When people know their purpose, they have found a reason to be alive. They find significance and meaning for their lives. Knowing your purpose gives you the desire to want to be alive.

It gives you a reason to grow, to expand, to develop and become a vibrant part of this world. Knowing your reason for being created stops you from merely existing. It motivates you to stop living a mediocre life, being average, and trying to survive like a wild animal.

Mankind's original purpose

A fundamental part of your purpose is leadership. Human beings were created to be leaders. God created humanity to have dominion.

He made us to have power, authority, and to be rulers. We were created to control and dominate the earth. Mankind was made to be kings over our environment. In the story of creation in the book of Genesis, it tells us so plainly why we were made.

> And God said, Let us make man in our image, after our likeness: and let them have dominion over the fish of the sea, and over the fowl of the air, and over the cattle, and over all the earth, and over every creeping thing that creepeth upon the earth.

> So God created man in his own image, in the image of God created he him; male and female created he them. And God blessed them, and God said unto them, Be fruitful, and multiply, and replenish the earth, and subdue it: and have dominion over the fish of the sea, and over the fowl of the air, and over every living thing that moveth upon the earth. (Gen. 1:26-28)

God gave Adam and Eve, humanity, dominion over the entire earth. God told them to subdue earth and have dominion over it. Let us look at these two words, subdue and dominion.

1. Dominion – to tread down, subjugate, to crumble off (5).
2. Subdue – (same meaning as dominion and also) to disregard, to conquer, violate (6).

God told mankind to subjugate all other species on this planet. Which means to totally subject something under your power. They were to make all animals be under their control to make the animal kingdom subjects unto the human kingdom.

God was instructing mankind to tread on them and make them crumble under their power if they did not want to obey their commands. He also told them to conquer them if they were to get out of line with humanity's authority. Mankind was created to be a kingdom of kings; a species of rulers and leaders.

In spite of mankind's initial role as being a kingdom of leaders, humanity lost their kingship. We lost our right to rule and govern the earth in the power and authority endowed unto us. This happened when Adam sinned against God and disobeyed His commandment in the Garden in Eden.

We lost our God-given right to rule and have dominion over the earth. Dr. Myles Munroe expressed this point when he wrote, "Therefore, the greatest need of mankind was identified by what he lost, he did not lose a religion or heaven, but rather a kingdom" (7).

How we lost our ruler-ship can be read and examined in Genesis 3. In verses 1 – 6, it gives us details of how our dominion was taken away from us. Satan, the serpent, went over to Adam and Eve and started a conversation.

It is interesting to note that the person Satan was speaking to was Eve and not Adam. We know that Adam was there during the time of the conversation, because in verse six of this chapter it says "and gave also unto her husband with her." From this statement it shows that Adam had to be in close proximity to Eve to receive the fruit that was given to him.

There is something else that can be pointed out, and that is during the course of this dialogue Adam did not say one word in asserting his God-given dominion and authority. Men, we must stand up and govern our houses in the authority that we have received from God. This is the place in scripture where Adam and Eve should have subdued and dominated the animal kingdom. The serpent should have been put in his rightful place.

The Bible declares that the serpent was talking to Eve about which trees in the garden they, Adam and Eve, were able to eat from. Then Eve responded to the Devil and told him that they could eat from every tree except for the one that is in the midst of the garden. We must observe how cunning the Devil truly is. He tricked Eve into thinking that God was trying to hold something from her enjoyment.

This is the same trick he uses today. He tells humanity that it is okay to fornicate and that you don't have to wait until you are married to have sex. He says it's not a big deal, you are in a monogamous relationship and it is like you are married.

In actuality, it does matter if you are not married and are having sex. God is not trying to stop you from having fun, enjoying sex. He wants to stop the pain that will eventually ravage your mind and maybe your body from having multiple sexual partners. Understand that each sexual relationship ties you to another person spiritually. When the time arrives for you to receive that one person who you are to marry, you cannot give yourself wholly over to that person because you have given yourself to somebody else.

Satan tricks people into thinking that God does not want us to enjoy this life. But in reality God is not trying to hurt us -- he wants to help us. God does not want us living contrary to his word because he understands that type of lifestyle has bad consequences of disease, death, and destruction.

Three Encounters that Happened to Eve

When Satan tricked Eve she encountered three types of sins. Genesis 3:6 declares, "And when the woman saw that the tree was good for food, and that it was pleasant to the eyes, and a tree to be desired to make one wise, she took of the fruit thereof, and did eat, and gave also unto her husband with her; and he did eat."

1. She saw the tree was good for food.

2. She saw it was pleasant to the eyes.
3. She saw it was a tree to be desired to make her wise.

When Eve believed the trick of the enemy, she stopped living by faith in God's word, "if you eat you die", and started living by sight. The three sins Eve encountered are the same three sins that occur every day in the heart of the ungodly. The Apostle John declares: "For all that is in the world, the lust of the flesh, and the lust of the eyes, and the pride of life, is not of the Father, but is of the world." (1 John 2:16)

The same three sins that run rampant in the earth are the same three sins that ran rampant in Eve. The lust of the flesh showed up, the tree was good for food. The lust of the eyes appeared, the tree was pleasant to the eyes. Then the pride of life was revealed, a tree to be desired to make one wise. Christians, be on guard for these three components of evil.

Then the Bible tells us that after they ate the fruit from the tree of knowledge of good and evil, their eyes were opened and they saw that they were naked, and they covered themselves with fig leaves. Chapter 3 of Genesis goes on to tell us that Adam and Eve hid from God. Then it explains the punishment that fell on humanity, creation, and the serpent because of their disobedience. It also shares with us that God put Adam and Eve out of the garden and placed a cherubim and a flaming sword at the east side of it to protect us from partaking of the fruit of the tree of life and staying in that sinful state for eternity.

When our authority was stripped from us, it was known as the fall of mankind. Our authority and power to rule the earth was given to Satan. Jesus called him "the prince of this world" in John 12:31. Then the apostle Paul said he is "the god of this age" (2 Cor. 4:4). Satan and sin dominated humanity, and the human race was in bondage under sin.

When mankind lost its authority and became subjects instead of rulers, we never lost the words God spoke to humanity, which was to have dominion and to subdue the earth. With humanity under the power of Satan, our understanding of dominion and subduing became twisted and perverted. After the fall of man, humanity's thinking became darkened and our understanding was tainted.

This is the reason why we have tyrants in leadership roles. This is also why we see many evil dictatorships, because mankind unconsciously wants to fulfill the original mandate from its Creator of dominating and subduing. Furthermore, this is why we have bosses violating their employees, wars, family feuds, prejudices, slavery, ethnic cleansing, and domestic violence because inwardly humanity is trying to manifest the command of God unknowingly through darkened and deceived minds.

Dr. Myles Munroe also declared, "The human spirit is possessed by the desire to dominate, rule, and control his personal private world and his environment. Man is in search of the ultimate governing power of dominion. The desire for power is inherent in the human spirit" (8). The deceived minds of mankind has taken this indwelling desire and perverted it, by trying to dominate and rule each other.

Believers regain purpose

Humanity has a reason to rejoice and to be exceedingly glad because of our Champion, the Lord Jesus the Christ. He took back humanity's authority of rulership and dominion from Satan. Mankind has regained the power of kingship through faith in Jesus. When He rose from the grave he conquered Satan and death and he received total power over heaven and earth.

Satan's authority has been stripped and he has been dethroned. Jesus Himself declared, "all power was given unto me in heaven and in earth" (Matt. 28:18). Christ overthrew the kingdom of darkness and took power and control over earth. He is NOW King over earth. He is the one in control and he has all governing power and authority.

Initial Steps to Restored Dominion – Salvation

Before anyone can start to regain their rightful position within this earth, they must be saved. They must understand that they have broken the laws of God and have sinned against Him. They also must know that they are in need of a Savior, and the only person that can save them from the wrath of God is his son Jesus the Christ.

Steps one through three are how a person gets saved. Steps four through seven are how a person matures in their faith in Jesus.

Step one. Repent. We have to turn from our wicked ways (thinking and actions) and ask God to forgive us of our sins. "I tell you, Nay: but, except ye repent, ye shall all likewise perish" (Luke 13:3).

Step two. Believe that Jesus Christ has died for your sins. "For even the Son of man came not to be ministered unto, but to minister, and to give his life a ransom for many" (Mark 10:45).

Step three. Believe in the resurrection of Jesus and confess that he is the Lord of your life. "That if thou shalt confess with thy mouth the Lord Jesus, and shalt believe in thine heart that God hath raised him from the dead, thou shalt be saved. For with the heart man believeth unto righteousness; and with the mouth confession is made unto salvation" (Rom. 10:9, 10).

Step four. Seek God in prayer so that you can be sent to a Bible-believing and teaching Church. We must assemble ourselves with other believers in Jesus Christ. "Not forsaking the assembling of ourselves together, as the manner of some is; but exhorting one another: and so much the more, as ye see the day approaching" (Heb. 10:25).

Step five. Start living your life by faith. Trusting and believing that God is going to do what He has promised. "But that no man is justified by the law in the sight of God, it is evident: for, The just shall live by faith" (Gal. 3:11).

Step six. Stay in constant communication with God the Father. You Must PRAY. "Praying always with all prayer and supplication in the Spirit, and watching thereunto with all perseverance and supplication for all saints" (Eph. 6:18).

Step seven. Read your Bible on a daily basis. Study it, memorize it, meditate on it, and do it. The way we live must change. The actions we do must change, and that starts with the renewing of our mind. We must change the way we think, and that happens when we spend time in God's Word. "And be not conformed to this world: but be ye transformed by the renewing of your mind, that ye may prove what is that good, and acceptable, and perfect, will of God" (Rom. 12:2).

Positional Authority

Everyone who has accepted Jesus as his or her Lord and Savior is in the body of Christ. Ephesians 1:22, 23 declares, "and hath put all things under his feet, and gave him to be the head over all things to the church, which is his body, the fullness of him that filleth all in all." Since Christians are the body of Christ, the church has through their faith in Jesus received their governing power and authority back.

Because of Christ, the powerful Almighty King, our kingship has been givrn back to us. Everything was put under the feet of Christ; it was put under our feet as well. Feet are the lowest part of the body and everything between the feet and the head is known as the body, and that is where the Church lies on Christ -- above his feet and underneath his headship.

Every principality, power, might, dominion, sickness, and devil is positioned under the control and rulership of Jesus Christ. We are above His feet and everything under his feet is subject unto Him. That would mean that everything is under our feet as long as we rely on Christ.

When Christ came to earth, he not only came to give us salvation but also to give us back our authority, our honor, and our rulership. He was born to reestablish humanity's dominion through the authority of the Kingdom of God. When people are saved, they become a part of a group of restored stewards and kings through the blood of Jesus. Our salvation produces restored dominion, restored authority, and restored leadership. Revelation 1:6 says "And hath made us kings and priest unto God and his Father; to him be glory and dominion for ever and ever Amen."

We went through this information to let you know that your purpose for being alive and being a Christian is connected to dominion and leadership. When you are a leader, numerous possibilities open up. Understand that your purpose is linked to the possibilities of the Almighty and Living God. You have the ability to do great and marvelous exploits for the glory of our Lord and God.

71

Each vision God reveals to you may be impossible in the eyesight of man but that is okay, because it is more than possible in the eyesight of our powerful God. Your vision positions you to continuously manifest your restored dominion that you have received through Christ Jesus.

God knows you

Jeremiah 1:5 is very encouraging. It says "Before I formed thee in the belly I knew thee; and before thou camest forth out of the womb I sanctified thee, and I ordained thee a prophet unto the nations." God told Jeremiah that 'before I formed you to go into your mother's womb I knew who I made you to be.' The word *knew* means observation, care, recognition, instruction, designation, and punishment (9).

God was telling Jeremiah 'before I created you, I cared for you and I observed the instruction and plans that I had for your life. I recognized that I designated you to be someone special on the earth. I also know the punishment I have prepared for you if you don't follow my plan.' God had a plan for Jeremiah's life before his parents knew they were having a baby.

God is saying the same thing to every person on this earth; he has a plan for their life. That plan is to do something special, a plan of greatness, but they have to come to him first. God has a plan and a purpose for your life. Stephen R. Covey wrote, "Deep within each one of us there is an inner longing to live a life of greatness and contribution – to really matter, to really make a difference" (10).

When you came to know Christ as your King, you were given power, authority, and influence. You were given the power through Christ to handle your world. You're blessed with the influence to talk to heads of governments, and the authority to govern your household with integrity and honesty. You were also given the leadership potential to run a successful business venture if that is part of your purpose.

Relationship Is Needed

You received power when you received Christ. Your purpose is connected to your salvation. You cannot fulfill your purpose for life without salvation in Jesus. The reason being, we have to be in right standing with our Creator before he reveals unto us our purpose. You cannot be in right standing with God if you are not saved and cleansed from your sins.

Only when a person is made pure by the blood of Jesus does he or she become in harmony with God, and then they are in right standing. Get a clear understanding of this statement; **We move into right standing with God when we confess with our mouth that Jesus is Lord and Savior and when we believe in our hearts that God has raised him from the dead (Ro. 10:9).** If you are not in right standing with God, he will not reveal to you your reason for being alive.

When you enter into a harmonious fellowship with God he will, over time, start to reveal to you your reason for being alive. He will start to show you visions that he desires for you to accomplish.

As you complete each vision he will demonstrate his power, his authority, and his glory through your life. You must understand this fact: God knew you before the foundation of the world. Before your parents knew you, God knew you. Before your parents knew they were having a beautiful baby, God ordained a plan for your life.

He recognized that he designated you for greatness. God has instructions to give to you for your life. He has a plan to guide you through the journey of life because he cares for you greatly. He also has a punishment waiting for you if you don't do his will for your life.

Only God knows what's in store for you. Only he knows the good pleasures he has waiting for you if you are obedient to his will. Get in fellowship with your Creator so he can reveal to you who you were created to be. Now, since you know you have a purpose to fulfill, your thinking has to change.

<u>Principles</u>

1. Your purpose is God's divine will for your life.

2. God must uncover for you what He has planned for your life.

3. When people know their purpose, they have a reason to be alive.

4. Fulfilling your purpose is a life-long pursuit.

5. Humanity was created to have dominion and power.

6. Mankind's dominion was given to Satan at the fall of mankind.

7. Every principality, power, might, dominion, sickness, and devil is positioned under the control and rulership of Jesus.

8. Your purpose is linked to the possibilities of the Almighty and Living God.

9. Jesus the Christ took humanity's authority back.

10. Your purpose is connected to you having dominion and being a leader.

*

Your thoughts are a crucial part to achieving your vision.

Your must transform your mind so your purpose can be fulfilled.

*

Chapter Three:
Renewed Thinking

A good man out of the good treasure of his heart bringeth forth that which is good; and an evil man out of the evil treasure of his heart bringeth forth that which is evil: for of the abundance of the heart his mouth speaketh.
-Luke 6:45-

The way a person thinks will determine the life they will live. Your thoughts produce your actions and the environment you live within. Your thoughts are powerful. Your thoughts influence your world. The Bible says, "For as he thinketh in his heart so is he" (Proverbs 23:7).

The two words that jump out in this passage of scripture is *thinketh* and *heart*. They are key to this verse. Their meanings are:

1. Thinketh – To split or open, to act as gatekeeper, to estimate (1).
2. Heart – Vitality (2)

Thinking deals with splitting and opening ideas and concepts. When you think, you are dissecting information to understand it fully. You have to be a gatekeeper guarding your mind. You must guard your mind against negative and evil thoughts.

77

You must also guard your mind against impure and unhealthy thoughts. You must always be on guard. Your capacity to think helps you estimate and judge the things that are going on around you.

All of our thinking is done where our vitality dwells. What is the vitality of mankind? Vitality means force and power. Vitality helps you grow and live your life. It is a place where your mentality can expand vigorously.

This place is called the mind. Your mind is what you must guard. Your mind is where you must be stationed as a gatekeeper. Proverbs 4:23 declares, "Keep thy heart with all diligence; for out of it are the issues of life."

The word *heart* in this verse is used for feelings, the will and intellect (3). It is important for us to understand that all three activities occur inside our minds. Our feelings and emotions are in our mind. Our will and our ability to determine what we want to do happen in our minds.

Our capacity to think and reason, which is our intellect, is found in our minds as well. We must guard our minds very diligently. A lot of the problems we encounter in life are due to the result of our negative thinking

Your thoughts produce your environment. This is the process: Thoughts produce thought patterns. Thought patterns become habitual thought patterns which breed actions. Actions repeated produce character. Character creates a lifestyle. Lifestyles produce consequences. Those consequences are manifested within our environments.

Four dimensions make up our environment:

1. **Physical** – The body we live in and the world we have
   access to through our five senses.
2. **Economic** – The capital resources we have access to which determines the house we live in, the car we drive, how well we can take care of our family financially.
3. **Social** – The different relationships we have in our lives.
4. **Spiritual** – How strong or weak our relationship is with God.

Our thoughts affect all four dimensions of our environments. Our thoughts will determine how well our bodies, are to a certain degree. Our thoughts will determine how much money we will be able to produce and have access to.

It is our thoughts that will determine the type of relationships we will have with our spouses, our children, our bosses, and with our co-workers and peers. Our thoughts will also determine how we will relate to God and the type of fellowship we will have with him. Our thoughts are very important to our lives and to our existence on this planet.

- Your thoughts are a key factor in the way you will live your life.
- Controlling your thoughts is a crucial part of manifesting your leadership. Your capacity to rule and lead will be based on the thoughts you allow to fill your mind.
- Every lifestyle, every character, every action, every word is a result of a thought.

Ideal

The way we think will determine how we see possibilities in life. When we think about what is possible in life, that is called our Ideal. Your Ideal is a model, a pattern, and a frame of reference you use when you try to determine if something is possible or impossible. Your Ideal helps you to "see" life. It is the lens we look through when we see our reality, and when we examine situations and possibilities.

Your Ideal was taught to you as you were being reared as a child. Your parents spoke to you and displayed before you what was possible and impossible in life. Your schoolteachers tutored you towards an area of possibilities or impossibilities. Then your experiences and circumstances spoke out to you, declaring what could be accomplished in your life. Your circumstances have a way of saying to you that you can't make it and that things will not get any better.

Understand that the reason why some people are wealthy is because someone told them and showed them that it was possible. The reason why some people have strong and vibrant bodies is because someone taught them and exposed them to a healthy lifestyle.

Many poor people were not taught and shown how to handle money, so financial freedom is considered impossible. The reason why a lot of people are not CEOs and entrepreneurs is because someone said and showed them that getting a job and being an employee was the only possible option.

Ideal Exchange

If you want to change your life and manifest your leadership, you have to change the way you think. You have to change your Ideal. You have to change what you think is possible and obtainable in life.

We need an "Ideal Exchange." It is the doing away with old limited thoughts and replacing them with thoughts of possibility. It is the process of exchanging old thoughts and thinking patterns for new and constructive ones.

We must exchange all limited, doubtful, and negative thinking with limitless and positive thoughts that are filled with faith. There is a book entitled *Christ Centered Therapy* and it declares, "Thoughts or beliefs leading to negative feelings and improper responses to life are identified as ineffective or dysfunctional" (4).

Moses had an Ideal Exchange

Moses is one of many within scripture that had an Ideal Exchange. In the Book of Exodus chapters 3 and 4, we see how he transformed from being a man with little confidence to a mighty vessel being used by the God of Glory. These two chapters of Exodus should be read and studied.

The Bible tells us that Moses had an encounter with the Living God on Mount Horeb, which is known as "the mountain of God" (Exod. 4:1). This was a defining moment in Moses' life. The decision he made in this encounter with God determined the direction he was going to go for the rest of his life.

The encounter Moses had with God came when he became content within a particular stage of life. Exodus 2:21 say "And Moses was content to dwell with the man and he gave Moses Zipporah his daughter." Moses was in a season in his life where he was living with and working for his father-in-law Jethro, who was a "priest of Midian" (Exod. 4:1).

The Bible says that Moses was content. The word *content* means to yield (5). Moses became humble. He humbled himself under the control of someone else. He submitted himself under another person's leadership and authority. When Moses yielded to Jethro's authority, God saw his submission and blessed him to lead a nation.

Understand that before God will use you in mighty ways, you have to be found faithful under another person's leadership and authority. You must yield under the mantle of authority that God has you under. Then over time, when God has seen that you have become humble and a need comes before his face, he will choose you to tend to it and he will use you in mighty ways for his glory (Exod. 2:23-25). There is a saying that is very encouraging which reads, "It is the crushed grape that yields the wine" (6). Charles E. Raven declared, "We must be broken into life" (7).

While Moses was taking care of his duties, tending to Jethro's sheep, God confronted Moses -- and that confrontation changed his life and altered the way he saw himself. Chapters 3 and 4 of Exodus is a conversation that God had with Moses. The dialogue deals with God choosing Moses to be an instrument of deliverance, to deliver the children of Israel out of the bondage of Egypt.

In this conversation, God is revealing to Moses his purpose for being created. A careful study of these two chapters will reveal to you some very interesting components concerning Moses' paradigm and the awesome power of God. As you study Chapters 3 and 4, you will see that Moses had three objections that he brought before God to show God he was not suited to fulfill his reason for being alive.

Moses' objections to purpose

1. The first objection shows us that Moses had a
   problem with self worth. He looks at himself as
   being unimportant. Moses says in Exodus 3:11
   "who am I, that I should go unto Pharaoh and
   that I should bring forth the children of Israel
   out of Egypt?"

   He was basically telling God that 'you are
   asking someone of minor significance to tell
   the king of Egypt what he must do'. Moses was
   saying 'I'm not a man of power or a person of
   influence and authority'. We see in the very
   next verse that God gave him a new look
   concerning his possibilities.

   Exodus 3:12 declares that God "said, Certainly
   I will be with thee; and this shall be a token
   unto thee, that I have sent thee: when thou hast
   brought forth the people out of Egypt, ye shall
   serve God upon this mountain."

   God was telling Moses that 'you don't have to
   worry about not being a person of power,
   because you will have my power because I will
   be with you'. When God reveals to you your
   purpose, it may look like it is impossible for
   you to accomplish. But don't fret' because God
   will give you his power to fulfill his desires.

2. The second objection uncovers for us that
   Moses was a person of little confidence.

Exodus 4:1 says "And Moses answered and said, But, behold, they will not believe me, nor hearken into my voice: for they will say, The Lord hath not appeared unto thee." Moses told the Lord of all creation, 'they (children of Israel) will not believe that I have talked to you and furthermore they won't even listen to what I have to say'.

Now Moses tells God this after God has already informed him in Exodus 3:18 that the children of Israel will listen to what he has to say. God does something to boost Moses' confidence -- He allowed Moses to do miracles (Exod. 4:2-9). When God has something for you to do, don't let a lack of confidence stand in your way to greatness.

3. The third objection shows us the reason why Moses had a self-worth problem and lacked confidence. Moses informs God that he is not an articulate person and he cannot speak well. He told God 'you do not want me to speak for you'.

'I do not speak well enough to be your messenger'. Exodus 4:10 says, "And Moses said unto the Lord, O my Lord, I am not eloquent, neither heretofore, nor since thou has spoken unto thy servant: but I am slow of speech and of a slow tongue."

Let us see how the Almighty responds to Moses' objection in verses 11 and 12, "And the Lord said unto him, Who hath made man's mouth? or who maketh the dumb, or deaf, or the seeing, or the blind? have not I the Lord? Now therefore go, and I will be with thy mouth, and teach thee what thou shalt say."

God was telling Moses not to worry about how articulate he was or about how well he spoke, because He was going to use his mouth and He would tell him what to say. That information is very encouraging, because when God wants to use you he looks past the requirements of this world and puts you in a position of greatness. God takes you as you are, broken and yielded.

Moses' thinking concerning his possibilities had to change. God **exchanged** his limited thinking to thoughts of optimism and possibility. God had to open his eyes to see a new horizon. God changed his Ideal.

Progress Toward Newness of Mind

Throw away those destructive thoughts about your past. You are not that person anymore. You are a new creature in Christ Jesus. Old things have passed away and behold all things are made new. That means you are new!

You are different now. You are not the same anymore. You are now a leader in the eyes of the Eternal God. We must fill our minds with constructive thoughts, so we can live our lives for the glory of our God.

There is another statement from *Christ Center Therapy* that applies here which reads "God never bypasses the mind; rather he works through it, transforming us by renewing of our minds"(8).

We have to reprogram our minds with optimism so we can change the way we think. Paul tells us in Philippians 4:8 the kinds of things we should fill our minds with. The verse declares, "Finally, brethren, whatsoever things are true, whatsoever things are honest, whatsoever things are just, whatsoever things are pure, whatsoever things are lovely, whatsoever things are of good report: if there be any virtue, and if there be any praise, think of these things."

We must do what the Bible declares in Ephesians 4:23 "and be renewed in the spirit of your mind." We have to renew our minds. Specifically, the spirit of our minds must be renewed. The word *renewed* means to renovate and to reform (9).

When something is being renovated, it is being restored to its proper working order. The idea is to make the item good again. We must restore our mind to its proper working order. We must reprogram ourselves to become leaders.

We have to restore our thinking back to the mind Adam and Eve had before the fall of man. Bring our minds back to the mindset of dominion, power, honor, and authority. We have to rebuild our thought patterns, so we can live our true roles as kings and priests unto the Almighty King of Glory.

In the book *Rediscovering the Kingdom* by Dr. Myles Munroe, he writes, "We must learn to think like kings again, to lay hold of the spirit and attitude of kings. This is why Kingdom Citizenship is really all about leadership. It is about kingship and ruling a domain" (10).

Paul said that this renovation project must be done in the spirit of our mind. In this verse, Paul is speaking of our disposition (11). Your disposition is your state of mind. It deals with our inclinations and our attitudes.

The state or condition of our minds needs to be renovated. Our inclinations and attitudes must be changed. How do we accomplish this renovation project? How can we exchange our Ideals?

Paul gives us a clue, also found in the book of Ephesians. He tells us in 5:19 how to do this. It says "speaking to yourselves in psalms and hymns and spiritual songs, singing and making melody in your heart to the Lord." We must encourage ourselves by speaking to ourselves.

If no one is encouraging you, you must tell yourself don't quit. If no one cheering for you, you say don't give up. You must speak to yourself.

Tell yourself, "I'm going to make it!" "I'm going to win." "Nothing is going to stand in my way or stop me." Say to yourself, "I am more than a conqueror." "I am an overcomer." "I am the head and not the tail." "I have abundance and not lack."

Internal Dialogue

Practice the concept of Internal Dialogue so you can continually encourage yourself. This is also known as self-talk. You have to talk to yourself so you can stay motivated.

You need to speak the word of God at all times. Repeat to yourself the word of God. Meditate and memorize the scriptures from the Bible. Repeat them mentally and out loud to yourself. God told Joshua:

> Only be thou strong and very courageous, that thou mayest observe to do according to all the law, which Moses my servant commanded thee: turn not from it to the right hand or to the left, that thou mayest prosper whithersoever thou goest. This book of the law shall not depart out of thy mouth; but thou shalt meditate therein day and night, that thou mayest observe to do according to all that is written therein: for then thou shalt make thy way prosperous, and then thou shalt have good success (Josh. 1:7-8)

Your internal communication is very important to fulfilling your purpose. No one talks to you more than you. So you have to make sure you are telling yourself the right things.

Search out godly people who have written books and read their literature. Listen to inspiring lectures so you can stay motivated. Find quotes from successful people and repeat them. Self-empowerment is a personal choice.

You Must Encourage Yourself

Prayer Produces Empowerment

Let us look at the other component to self-encouragement. This other side of encouragement is seen in the life of King David of Israel. In 1 Samuel 30:6 - 8 we find these words:

> And David was greatly distressed; for the people spake of stoning him, because the soul of all the people was grieved, every man for his sons and for his daughters: but David encouraged himself in the Lord his God. And David said to Abiathar the priest, Ahimelech's son, I pray thee, bring me hither the ephod. And Abiathar brought thither the ephod to David. And David enquired at the Lord, saying, Shall I pursue after this troop? Shall I overtake them? And he answered him, Pursue: for thou shalt surely overtake them, and without fail recover all.

90

Let us acquire a little background information pertaining to this text. David and his men arrived at the city of Ziklag, where they were living. When they arrived at the city, it was on fire and all of their relatives (wives, sons and daughters) had been taken captive by the Amalekites. At this point all of David's men turned on him and wanted to kill him, because they felt that this was all David's fault.

We can somewhat understand the position David was in when he had to encourage himself in the Lord. His city and home were on fire, his wives were in captivity along with his soldiers' families, and to top it all off his soldiers wanted to kill him. Talking about a depressing situation.

The Bible says, "David was greatly distressed" (1 Sam. 30:6). David's life was crumbling onto his shoulders. The pressures of life were pressing upon him. Can you image the pain, the anxiety, and the sorrow he was feeling during that time?

The Bible tells us the actions of David. He did not try to commit suicide. He didn't go out and get high to relieve his pain. The Bible declares "but David encouraged himself in the Lord his God" (1 Sam. 30:6).

David knew that the only person that could help him was God Almighty. "David enquired at the Lord" the Bible tells us. *Enquire* means to request (12). David encouraged himself by going to pray.

He talked to the Lord about his situation. He went to God to request an answer on how to handle this problem he was facing. The Word of God says that God gave David counsel so he could get out of this horrible situation.

When the pressures of life are weighing you down, go and talk to the Lord. Go and inquire of him, and receive counseling from the all knowing and all-powerful God. When the Lord gives you directions and tells you to do something, it is to strengthen you and to make you strong. God wants to help us through hard and difficult situations.

External Dialogue

Our next step is to add external dialogue, to look for people who are living their purpose and are striving for their vision, and start mingling with them. It is important to be with people who are going places.

Befriend people who are doing what you want to do. They will encourage you and motivate you to strive to accomplish your vision. When you surround yourself with people of vision, significant strides will be made towards reaching your goals. This is why we must attend a local church fellowship.

We must be around people who are striving to be holy and who are striving to be Christ-like, because this is what we want to do. The Bible declares in Hebrews 10:25, "Not forsaking the assembling of ourselves together, as the manner of some is; but exhorting one another: and so much, as ye see the day approaching."

Strivers must be around strivers. Overcomers must be around overcomers. It's okay if you are striving currently and your associates have strived and achieved. It's also okay if you are overcoming and they have overcome because they can share with you their trials, tribulations, experiences, and successes to help you along your path toward fulfillment.

Remember what the Apostle proclaimed in Philippians 4:13, which is "I can do all things through Christ, which strengtheneth me." That word *strenghteneth* means to empower (13). You can do all things because Christ has empowered you to overcome the world and your problems, because he overcame the world. You have been empowered to succeed. You have been empowered to have victory in your life.

It may be difficult at first to renew your mind, to stop thinking thoughts full of doubt and despair. Remember, you have been given power to change your thinking. You have power to receive a new outlook on life and to reprogram your Ideal from impossibility to possibility. We as Christians must be optimistic people.

If no one has hope, we must have hope. If no one sees tomorrow in a positive light, we must see it in a positive one. If no one sees opportunity, we should be able to see opportunity. Those limited states of mind we are accustomed to must be removed and destroyed for the glory of the Living God.

All states of mind can be changed and removed. Just like they can be changed and removed they can also be added, expanded, and enhanced. We have to change and remove negative thinking and add positive and optimistic thinking. Cultivate the mindsets that are going to help you fulfill your vision.

Cultivation of Positive Mindsets

Here are a few we should focus on cultivating.

1. Possibility/Optimism – Start believing that reaching your vision is possible. Begin memorizing scriptures to help you on this journey. Here are a couple of verses to remember:

   Mark 9:23 "All things are possible to him that believeth."

   Mark 10:27 "With God all things are possible."

   Before you can do anything, you have to believe that it is possible. You have to believe that it is attainable. See your purpose and your vision as something that is possible, and they can be achieved.

2. Desire – This is the beginning position on the way to success. Desire is a strong, intense longing for something. It is the fuel that is needed so you can continue in spite of the obstacles. This is essential for you to reach your destiny.

   You need a strong desire to reach your vision and to fulfill your purpose. Yet this desire is secondary to the desire you must have to please God. This desire is foundational to your existence.

   He is the one who created your purpose and revealed to you your vision. Keep this scripture in mind from Psalms 37:4 – "Delight thyself also in the Lord; and he shall give thee the desires of thine heart."

3. Faith – This is being in a state of expectancy. You need to have a sense of expectation. Faith is another key you must have as you develop leadership. You must expect to see your vision realized.

   There should be no doubt in your mind of its completion. It is not a matter of if; it is a matter of when. You must know beyond a shadow of a doubt that the vision God has given you will come to pass. Declare fervently to yourself Hebrews 11:1 – "Now faith is the substance of things hoped for, the evidence of things not seen."

4. Determination – This word come from the word *determine*. To have determination you must determine or rather make a choice. You must determine what you are striving after.

    You have to make a decision about your life. Become a person who does not mind making decisions. Learn how to make decisions quickly in the heat of battle with a cool, calm, and collective frame of mind. This can be accomplished with much practice.

    You have to determine how you are going to live your life. Will you be mediocre and average, or are you going to be superb and above average? That choice is up to you.

    You have to make up in your mind what kind of person you are going to be. Only you can make that decision. Only you can decide which path you are going to take in life.

We must focus on cultivating these states of mind. As you develop them, they will seep down into the recesses of your mind, moving from your conscious to the subconscious. The conscious portion of your mind is where you are able to think about your thoughts and actions. On the other hand, your subconscious is where your thoughts are embedded in your mind. Those thoughts then propel you to do their correlating actions almost automatically.

We want encouraging and positive thoughts to move to our subconscious. When that happens, those thoughts will spring forward automatically, with no strong conscious effort on our behalf. The more we are persistent in changing our lives to live our purpose, the more tenacious we will be in renewing and reprogramming our minds.

Do not be like those who are mediocre and allow anything to fill their minds. You must fight to have an optimistic view on life. The mediocre and the average take the path of least resistance. They do not want to fight for their vision and their purpose. They do not want to progress towards a brighter future.

But the overcomers and the achievers stay in the fight even when the whole world is on the opposing side. Remember, Jesus faced the same type of situation. His friends (disciples) left him. The Jews wanted him crucified and the Roman government put him on the Cross. People who follow Jesus Christ should not worry when people disagree with them, because people disagreed with Jesus.

We must have the mindset that as long as we are still alive we will continue to pursue God's will. As long as we are alive we have a chance to win. As long as we have a chance there is still hope. **Hope is what is needed to bring your dreams to pass.**

Remember, you have to work on your mind before you can work on your environment. Everything moves from the internal, spiritual, imagination, and dreams of a person. Then they are manifested and actualized in the external physical world. We have to realize that our thinking affects our actions and our actions will take us to our vision.

Principles

1. Your thoughts influence your world.

2. Your thoughts are a key factor in the way you live.

3. Our thoughts will determine how we will relate to God and the type of fellowship we will have with Him.

4. Your thoughts concerning what is possible or impossible were taught to you.

5. The reason why many people are poor and poverty-stricken is because someone told and modeled before them that it was impossible to have financial freedom.

6. Our minds must be reprogrammed to possibility thinking.

7. You must encourage yourself.

8. We have been empowered to succeed and to have a victorious life.

9. Christians must be optimistic people.

10. Righteous thoughts help you fulfill your purpose and accomplish your vision.

STEPHEN D. OWENS

*

**Actions are the key to opening the door to
accomplishment.**

Without actions, all visions wither and die.

*

Chapter Four:
Actions for Manifestation

Even so faith, if it hath not works, is dead, being alone.
-James 2:17-

Action is the next element we must focus on while we are on the road to achievement and accomplishment. Your actions are a crucial step that must be addressed if you want to fulfill your purpose. Nothing happens until your actions are put into motion.

Nothing moves until action propels it in a certain direction. The motivational speaker Anthony Robbins wrote, "Action is the catalyst for every great success. Action is what produces results" (1). Always remember, **your actions are the outward display of your internal decisions.**

You declare your thoughts through your actions. If you want to know how a person thinks, observe his or her actions and behavior. This will tell you a lot about an individual. Your actions expose your thoughts and the mind controls the body.

Therefore, your thinking produces your action. Sinful, wrong, and undesired actions are the result of sinful, wrong, and unproductive thoughts. You are in your actions, character, and lifestyle what you are in your thoughts. To produce a desired result (action) you must fill your mind with correct and positive thoughts.

We must look at life the way the Apostle Paul did when he saw obstacles as when he was trying to progress in life. He declares in Philippians 3:14; "I press toward the mark for the prize of the high calling of God in Christ Jesus."

Paul said he pressed toward something. The Apostle was pursuing a goal. He was in forward motion towards a finish line. Paul says he is taking action to reach a mark.

A mark is a goal, a finish line, or a bull's eye. He is moving forward to reach a goal so he can receive a prize. Paul is telling us that he took action to move forward towards a goal so he can receive a reward.

This is the same thing we must do. We must take action to reach the goals that God has ordained for our lives. Once the job is completed and the goal has been reached, a reward will be given to us for our faithfulness by God for reaching his vision for our life.

The flow of thoughts to actions:

**Thoughts - habitual thought patterns -
actions - repeated actions - character
(YOU!)**

You must take steps to reach your vision and to fulfill your purpose. Now is the time to take steps to manifest your leadership. You must move forward to reach your goals. Each goal reached is a milestone closer to manifesting your vision and revealing your kingship to the world.

The book of Proverbs gives us wise counsel concerning the reward for taking action. Another word for action is *work*. Proverbs 12:14 NLT states, "hard work brings rewards." The Living Bible translation for Ecclesiastes 11:4 is very encouraging as well. It says, "If you wait for perfect conditions, you will never get anything done."

Don't wait for everything to be perfect. **TAKE ACTION NOW.** Stop sitting around waiting for the stars to be aligned just right before you do something. Do not waste your time -- it is very precious.

Action is what's needed to get to your vision. It is the workhorse that will carry you to victory. You have to put effort into it so you can achieve the vision. Progress is achieved when action is applied to your plan.

As declared earlier, your body responds to your mind. Take control of your mind and you take control of your body. Take control of your body and you take control of your actions.

Take control of your actions and you take control of your future. As you become more responsible for your future, your authority, honor, and leadership will be displayed for the glory of God.

You **<u>MUST CHOOSE</u>** to produce actions that will help you reach your vision. You cannot allow your body to dictate to you what you should do. Do not allow your cravings and your feelings to control your body and your actions. *You* control your body and *you* tell your body what it will have and what it needs.

Just because your body craves drugs does not mean you have to give it drugs. Just because your body craves a touch from someone else's spouse does not mean you should do or allow it. Or just because your body craves more food when you KNOW you have eaten enough does not mean you have to give in.

When our cravings and feelings are dictating our actions, something is wrong. This is an external-to-internal process, and this does not work when you want to reach your vision. This only works to give you short-term solutions to stop your cravings.

When you give in and feed your cravings in order to stop them, this only makes it grow stronger for the next time. Then when these feelings show up again, this time they have has intensified. Stop the cravings by starving them to death. If you don't feed it, it will die.

Only feed that which you want to grow and live -- like your family, your purpose, your vision, and healthy actions. Those things are fed by working on them. You have to improve them and make them better so they can prosper and be fruitful.

Tell your body how to act so you can produce the actions you want. Do not allow your body to run rampant doing whatever it pleases. Take control of your body. Take control now.

Apostle Paul's Perspective on Self-mastery:

The Apostle Paul gives us wise advice once again that we should heed. The Apostle was counseling the church at Corinth concerning taking authority over their bodies. This information is helpful on our journey as well. He said

> Know ye not that they which run in a race run all, but one receiveth the prize? So run, that ye may obtain. And every man that striveth for mastery is temperate in all things. Now they do it to obtain a corruptible crown; but we an incorruptible. I therefore so run, not as uncertainly; so fight I, not as one that beateth the air: but I keep under my body, and bring it into subjection: lest that by any means, when I have preached to others, I myself should be a castaway. (1 Cor. 9:24-27).

In these verses, the Apostle is informing the brethren at Corinth about the process a person has to go through when that individual is running within a race. Paul compares the race that an athlete runs to the race that believers run. He tells us that the person who runs within the physical game runs to win a corruptible crown.

The athlete competes to receive something that will wither away. People who run within the game of life in order to become more Christ-like run to receive an incorruptible crown. This is a crown that will never fade or wither away. In verse 25 the Apostle gives us astounding insight into the concept of self-mastery. "And every man that striveth for the mastery is temperate in all things" (1 Cor. 9:25).

Paul said, "every man that striveth for the mastery is temperate in all things." Let us try to gain an understanding into this concept. The word *striveth* means to struggle, to compete for a prize, to contend with an adversary, and to endeavor to accomplish something (2).

The word *mastery* suggests to have control and to dominate. When a person is *temperate,* he exercises self-restraint (3). Let's translate this verse and let us see if we can get a clearer picture of what the Apostle Paul is trying to paint for us.

Translation:

1. "Every person that struggles for control and dominance while contending with his adversary will exercise self-restraint in all things."
2. "Everyone that is endeavoring to accomplish something so he can obtain the prize of control and dominion will exercise self control in all things."

When we are engaged in a battle over a certain area in our life, that battle makes us strong so we will be able to wage war on other situations we are facing. During those times when we are fighting to conquer and dominate our ungodly appetites, we are building our strength so we will be able to wrestle against the dark forces that oppose us in other areas in our lives.

Then we see in verse 27 Paul becomes aggressive in his stand to not allow his body to dictate his actions. He said: "But I keep under my body, and bring it into subjection: lest that by any means, when I have preached to others, I myself should be a castaway."

Paul said, "I keep under my body." The phrase to *keep under* in the Greek means to subdue one's passions (4). Paul told the church at Corinth that he subdues the passions that his body has. He controls his passions; his passions do not control him. Paul dominated his body; his body did not dominate him.

You have to make your body be subjected to the will and word of God whether it feels like being obedient or not. That means, preacher, that you must study and prepare yourself to deliver the inspired word of God. Business owner, you have to make those calls for your next meeting, even if you are tired. You must push yourself to fulfill your purpose even when your body does not want to move.

Out-of-control actions and behaviors are the result of out-of-control thoughts. As declared earlier, you

must fill your mind with scripture, positive
affirmations and inspiring quotes.

We must understand that we cannot merely listen
to and speak these concepts, and then not apply them
to our daily lives. Information without application is
worthless to us. To succeed in manifesting your
purpose and vision, you must apply what you learn.

People believe that information is power. They
are partially correct when they make that statement.
Information does have power, but it is potential power.
Not until that information is acted upon and applied to
one's situation does it become real power.

Anthony Robbins made another great
statement, which is "Knowledge alone is only potential
power, and until it comes in the hands of someone who
knows how to take effective action, it will remain
dormant. In fact, the literal definition of the word
power is 'the ability to act'" (5).

Information + No Action = Potential Power

Information + Action = Real Power

We must receive the warning given by the
Apostle James: "But be ye doers of the word, and not
hearers only, deceiving your own selves" (Jam. 1:22).
We have to be doers, not just listeners. If we do not
apply the word of God the only person we are truly
deceiving is ourselves. The word *doers* means
performer (6).

We must continually perform those Biblical principles and positive concepts of which we are speaking. The word *deceive* means to *delude* (7). This word means to mislead the minds. We must be performers, doing what we believe to be correct and true. We must make take action in our lives by making our bodies perform the concepts we have learned.

It is no good to only listen to inspiring messages. There is no profit in merely hearing motivational material and not applying it to your life. When we do not apply the concepts we have heard, we are misleading our minds. We are lying to ourselves. We are tricking ourselves into believing that we are going to do something when in actuality we are not.

One of the worst acts you can do is lie to yourself. Do not mislead yourself. Do not play tricks on your mind -- that's cruel. Do the concepts that you have read and studied in the word of God. Do the things that will further your growth and development.

Principle of Sowing and Reaping

We must also work with the principle of sowing and reaping so we can capitalize on our potential for greatness. The principle of sowing and reaping is also known by another phrase, the law of seedtime and harvest. The Bible declares in the book of Galatians, "for whatsoever a man soweth, that shall he also reap" (Gal. 6:7). The basic concept is this; whatever you put out is what you are going to get back.

Stephen R. Covey calls this concept the "law of the harvest." Covey declared, "There is a 'law of the harvest' that governs human character, human greatness and all human relationship" (8). What we give will be given back to us. When you love others, others will love you. When you extend a hand, someone will extend a hand to you.

Now understand that the one you extend these actions to may not be the same person who reciprocates those actions. We should not look for repayment for the deeds we do from people we have helped. We understand that when we do something good it shall come back to us, but it may come back from another person. "Be not deceived; God is not mocked: for whatsoever a man soweth, that shall he also reap" (Gal. 6:7).

We must work in a constructive manner with this eternal principle. Whether you believe this principle is correct or incorrect, it will operate anyway. This principle is always at work, so why not use it to help yourself? Why not use it so you can prosper and reach your full potential as being a king and a leader?

Genesis 8:22 says, "while the earth remaineth, seedtime and harvest, and cold and heat, and summer and winter, and day and night shall not cease." For as long as the earth exists, someone will be planting and reaping a harvest. The creator of humanity–God–has established sowing and reaping in this world. It is an eternal law of creation. It is a universal and unchangeable law of the Living God.

You will either work with it for your benefit or it will work against you for your downfall. Choose today which side of this law you will be on. Will you cooperate with it, or will you live and act as if it does not exist? Make your choice. You will either work with it or it will work against you.

The first place this law can be applied is in the inner part of our being. Use this law on your mind and on your thinking first. Then move onto your actions and finally your circumstances. We must focus on the inside-out approach to life.

As we start to sow the word of God and positive affirmations into our thoughts, this information will eventually become planted into our minds. We have to sow seeds of encouragement into our thoughts with the concept of internal dialogue.

As you sow these words and concepts you will start to reap positive thought patterns. The more those thought patterns are meditated upon, the more they will start to become habitual and consistent. Followed carefully, the more you sow these habitual thoughts through contemplation, the more you will begin to reap their correlating actions.

The more you work on your thoughts, the more positive results you will harvest in your life. (To study more about your thoughts, review Chapter Three.) While the law of sowing and reaping is working to your benefit, make sure you incorporate the principle of cultivation and pruning.

What does it mean to cultivate? It means to *carefully observe, to tend to, to water and to feed.* Pruning means to *remove or to cut away.* While you are sowing positive thought into your mind, you must be careful because your old destructive thoughts may creep into your mind without any warning. You have to continually observe your thoughts.

When you notice that a thought is of a negative nature, quickly attack it and remove it by speaking to yourself the word of God. Paul tells us we should continually be in the process of "casting down imaginations, and every high thing that exalteth itself against the knowledge of God, and bring into captivity every thought to the obedience of Christ" (2 Cor. 10:5).

We are encouraged to always be in the process of "casting down imagination... that exalteth itself against the knowledge of God." We must be ready to demolish or cast down every act or process of reasoning that exalts itself against the knowledge of God and the vision he has revealed.

Therefore, every thought that appears in your mind to fight against the will of God for your life, you must be demolished and cast out of your mind. Paul tells us to take authority over every thought and make it submit to the Lord Jesus the Christ.

The two principles of sowing and reaping, and cultivation and pruning, are laws that can be found in a naturalistic atmosphere, like a farm. What happens on a farm? A farmer sows or scatters seeds in the field in the springtime. This is the aspect of planting.

Then, on a continuous basis, he waters and tends to the field. He also works with the weather to help feed his seeds. This is a concept God uses in our lives so we can grow and mature into the leaders he wants us to become. He works with the rain (hard times and trouble) that falls within our lives to produce the fruitful character of a true follower of Christ.

When the farmer sees that his seeds are beginning to bud, he observes them to see if part of the plant is withering and dying. If so, that portion is pruned and removed from the plant. The reason he does this is so that the decaying part does not affect the portion of the plant that is vibrant and growing.

The farmer goes through this process of pruning and cultivating all summer. Then in the fall it is time for the harvest. Now at reaping time the plants are healthy and ready to be picked and consumed, so the farmer goes to the field and gathers the harvest.

The Cycle of Seedtime and Harvest

This is what we are doing in our lives as we develop our roles of leadership. We are the farmers sowing God's word into our hearts and minds so we can reap a positive harvest of godly actions. The positive actions we reap from the encouraging words we have sown will push us towards our vision and our purpose.

When we find a positive action that pushes us forward, we must turn it into a habit. We want to do that positive action repeatedly until it becomes automatic. The only way something becomes automatic is if we do it on a habitual basis, day in and day out. When you practice an action continually and make it a habit, and you perform it automatically that action has reached your subconscious mind. Understand that when an action reaches your subconscious, the action is done almost without any conscious effect.

What we are doing is mastering the actions that will help us fulfill our purpose and actualize our vision. The next step we must take is to find another action that is good and positive, and then master that one too. We must repeat this process over and over, finding propelling actions and mastering them by making them habitual.

As we work on this process, we are operating within the principle known as the "Habit of Doing". This is the art of finding and performing positive habitual actions on a constant basis. John Dryden declared, "We first make our habits, and then our habits make us" (9). Dryden's statement echoes a quote by Blaise Pascal, which is "The strength of a man's virtue should not be measured by his special exertions, but by his habitual acts" (10).

Here are a few positive actions to turn into habits to develop your leadership:

1. Get serious about having a prayer life. "Pray without ceasing" (1 Thes. 5:17).

2. Study and meditate on the Bible. "Study to shew thyself approved unto God, a workman that needeth not to be ashamed, rightly dividing the word of truth" (2 Tim. 2:15).

3. Read and research information about your vision. "The cloke that I left at Troas with Carpus, when thou comest, bring with thee, and the books, but especially the parchments" (2 Tim. 4:13).

4. Plan weekly, monthly, and yearly objectives. "Ponder the path of thy feet, and let all thy ways be established" (Prov. 4:26).

5. Start comparing your results to your goals and plans. "I have fought a good fight, I have finished my course, I have kept the faith" (2 Tim. 4:7).

6. Start exercising spiritually, physically, and mentally. "For bodily exercise profiteth little: but godliness is profitable unto all things" (1Tim. 4:8).

Now there is one essential action we must learn and apply if we want to manifest our vision and fulfill our purpose, and that is the art of communication.

Principles

1. All actions are outward displays of internal decisions.

2. Actions are the results of thoughts.

3. Action is the workhorse that will carry you to victory.

4. Take control of your mind and you take control of your body.

5. Do not merely listen to the Word of God, do what it teaches.

6. One of the worst things you can do is lie to yourself.

7. Sowing and reaping is an eternal law of God.

8. Cultivate positive actions and prune destructive ones.

9. Repeat positive actions so they can become habitual.

10. Habitual actions will move you towards your future.

*

Communication is an art that must be practiced.

No one will buy into your vision if you cannot communicate it effectively.

*

Chapter Five:
The Art of Communication

*Let your conversation be always full of grace,
seasoned with salt, so that you may know how to
answer everyone.
-Colossians 4:6-*

Up to this point, you have learned that your vision in life must come from God. Then we talked about how your purpose for being alive is to do the will of God. Next, you learned that in order to reach your vision and fulfill your purpose, your thoughts have to change. In the previous chapter you were told that your actions are extremely important in manifesting the vision and your leadership.

In this chapter we are going to focus on the communication skills you will need as you lead. Learning the art of communication will be a necessity if you want to achieve your vision. You must have the ability to communicate your vision to people. Expressing your vision orally and on paper is essential. The beginning portion of Proverbs 12:14 says, "A man shall be satisfied with good by the fruit of his mouth."

Remember, being a leader deals with mobilizing, energizing and inspiring people. Therefore, because you are a leader you have to have the ability to do these three functions of leadership. These functions are accomplished through communication.

Keep in mind Colossians 4:6 "Let your speech be always with grace, seasoned with salt, that you may know how ye ought to answer every man." Stephen R. Covey also encourages us with these words "Simply put – at its most elemental and practical level – leadership is communicating to people their worth and potential so clearly that they come to see it in themselves" (1).

Communication is an Art

Communication is an art, not a science. A science is something that is concrete. It is when you do something a certain way and you get a certain result every single time the act is performed. When something is a science, no matter what situation you are in, if you do the action it will turn out the same way every time. Dealing with people and communication is an art.

When talking to a group of people everyone has heard the same words at the same time, yet the information that they heard will not produce the same actions. When you say something to one person, he or she may interpret it totally different then the other person you told the exact same words. This happens because every one's mental makeup is different. Everyone thinks differently.

We analyze information differently. God did not make humanity from a cookie cutter, with everyone being the same. We have the ability to understand and interpret things in a variety of different ways. This is the workmanship of a great and awesome Creator, to have the ability to make a creation so vastly different but at the same time so accurately the same. God is awesome!

Trust - The Foundation of Communication

The foundation of all communication is trust. People must trust you before they will follow you. They must feel that you have their best interest in mind when you are making your decisions.

In order for you to be trusted, you must be trustworthy. Trustworthiness is a result of your character and lifestyle. It has less to do with the words you say and more to do with your lifestyle. Your lifestyle is the basis of trustworthiness.

If people don't trust you, they will not believe in you. If they don't believe in you, they will not buy into your vision. If they do not buy into your vision, they will not support your endeavors. Your vision needs the support of other people for it to be reality. You need their physical energy and economic power.

A Trustworthy Leader

Among other qualities, to be a good leader you must be open, transparent and approachable.

Open. You should be able to share some of your failures and successes. That means you must tell the board members about the financial records and any other problems that may arise. People who follow you should know the direction in which God is leading you. You also must speak candidly and frankly about situations as they happen. Be like Solomon when he said, "for my mouth shall speak truth" (Prov. 8:7).

Transparent. You cannot hide behind the mask of your position, your pastorate, your board status of CEO or your financial position because you are the dominant breadwinner of your family. Your people must know who you are. They need to be able to see the real you. If you make a mistake, admit it. Handle it and move on.

Approachable. Your people should be able to talk to you. Your children must be able to come to you when their lives are in a mess. People should not leave feeling worse than they did when they came and opened up to you and exposed their problems. Do not browbeat your people.

Your followers should not leave feeling belittled and subservient to you because you made them feel lower than you. Always remember, you are only as great as the people you lead. Keep this formula in mind:

**Openness + Transparency + Approachableness =
Trustworthy Leadership**

The foundation of communication is trust, not speech.

Internal and External Trust

You must be able to trust you before others will learn to trust you. There are two types of trust -- internal and external. We will focus on the internal trust first, then we will move to external trust. We must first start by building trust in ourselves.

Now, do not misunderstand. This is not a prideful self-righteous trust nor is it a self-centered trust. This is not the type of trust where you believe that you can rely on yourself for salvation, protection, well-being, and security. Only God has the ability to do that for us.

Psalms 118:8 declares "it is better to trust in the Lord than to put confidence in man." Then Psalms 4:5 says "offer the sacrifices of righteousness, and put your trust in the Lord." The word *trust* from this verse means refuge, be confident and sure trust (2). The one who has the power to totally protect you and to be your refuge is God. He is the only person you can put your total confidence in.

The trust that is being promoted here is for individuals to start practicing a lifestyle of integrity. It is when you are confident in knowing that when you say something you are going to do it. This is when you have the ability to keep your word.

Blaine Lee expressed this truth when he declared, "Integrity means we are committed to matching words, feeling, thoughts, and action so that we live with congruence and without duplicity" (3). As you keep your word, you will start developing integrity and you will begin to establish a good character. Read what the word of God declares about integrity.

"Judge me, O Lord; for I have walked in mine integrity" (Ps. 26:1).

"The integrity of the upright shall guide them" (Prov. 11:3).

"The just man walketh in his integrity: his children are blessed after him" (Prov. 20:7).

When you are building your trustworthiness, you begin to keep your word no matter the situation. This is when you can say no, and mean no, and stay in the position of *no* until things change. Or when you say that you agree with something or someone, and you will continue to agree no matter who disagrees with you for it.

Matthew 5:37 declares "But let your communication be, Yea, yea; Nay, nay: for whatsoever is more than these cometh of evil." This is what it means to have integrity. It is when your yes is yes and your no is no and you will not waver simply because someone does not like your decision. George Washington made a great statement, "I hope I shall possess firmness and virtue enough to maintain what I consider the most enviable of all titles, the character of an honest man" (4).

We have to arrive at this level of maturity, where we believe that we will do the words that we have spoken. You must believe that you will complete the goals and responsibilities you agreed to. You must develop the confidence that you will do what is right and correct no matter who is around or who is not there to see your performance.

Imitators of God

When we live our lives with integrity, we are living and acting in the same manner as God. God is a God of integrity. He always keeps his word. When God gives us a promise, you can count on it coming to pass. In the book of Isaiah it says in 55:11 "so shall my word be that goeth forth out of my mouth: it shall not return unto me void, but it shall accomplish that which I please, and it shall prosper in the thing whereto I sent it."

When God says something is going to happen, it will happen. This is the way we must be. When we say we are going to perform a task, there should not be any questions asked concerning our ability and commitment in fulfilling the task at hand. We have to walk our talk and do what we have said. This is very important.

Get a clear understanding of this: God always keeps his word and he always makes his promises come true. The Bible tells us to be followers of God. Ephesians 5:1 says "be ye therefore followers of God as dear children." The word *follower* in the Greek means to imitate (5). When we imitate someone, we do the actions they do. We act the way they act by mimicking their actions.

This is the way we are to live as Christians. We are to mimic the demeanor and actions of our Lord and Savior Jesus Christ. Our character must match the character of Jesus. When people observe our behavior, they should see the way Jesus would be acting in that same situation. When the world sees our kingship being displayed, they should see the deeds and mannerism of the King of Kings.

How Do We Create Internal Trust?

1. Start small. Declare you are going to complete an assignment, then accomplish it.
2. Now find another job to do and complete that one too. But this time the task must be larger than the first one.
3. Then repeat this process over and over again.

This process should seem familiar -- it is the "Habit of Doing". We are applying it to the practice of keeping our words and promises. Each task that you complete should be a goal that you have set for yourself in order to accomplish your vision.

This process builds your trustworthiness. The more you keep your word the larger your trustworthiness will grow and the more integrity you will establish. Integrity is nothing more than you doing what you said you were going to do. You are keeping your word congruent with your actions.

Transition to External Trust

What begins to happen over time is that people will begin to witness that you are the kind of person who keeps their word, and people will start to trust you. When people see you make goals and then accomplish them, they begin to see you are a person they can trust. Over time, internal trustworthiness creates external trust.

When external trustworthiness starts to play a role in your life, people who are in your circle of influence (friends, family and associates) will began to trust you. Then as these people continue to trust you and in your ability to keep your word, they will start to feel comfortable with you and they will tell others about you and your ability. As a result of this process, your circle of trust will expand and grow.

As your circle expands, your influence with these individuals will grow as well. Trust is the foundation of communication. It is also the foundation for influence. You must be a person of influence to encourage others to work with you towards your goals.

When people believe that you have their best interests at heart and that you are a person of integrity, your communication with them will be effective and your influence with them will grow. **Keep in mind: Internal Trust produces External Trust, and Internal Integrity produces External Integrity!**

Remain Focused

We must be an army of one before we can be an army of many. Developing our trustworthiness is essential for leadership. We must develop our integrity and learn how to communicate effectively. Start establishing a one-person army before you start recruiting people.

Change always starts with us first. If you want to change your community ,start by changing you and your household. To change your work environment, you must change *you* first while you are still in that environment.

Change is highly contagious. When one thing changes, it affects everything that is around it. The change will force its environment to change.

To be an effective leader and to be a person who is a change catalyst, one must learn how to communicate. Peter F. Drucker wrote in his book *The Effective Executive,* "Effectiveness, in other words, is a habit, that is, a complex of practices. And practices can always be learned" (6). Mastering the art of communication will help you express your vision to the world.

There are three areas of communication. The first is internal communication, which we know as internal dialogue. The second area of communication is the written word. The last area is oral communication. We must continually work on these three areas so our influence can expand.

Three Types of Communication

1. Internal communication. You must be able to tell yourself clearly what you want done. You have to have the ability to express your vision in detail so you can understand it first. Once you understand the vision clearly, you will have the ability to express the vision to others. If you don't understand and cannot comprehend your vision, most people will feel lost when you are trying to explain it to them. To review this form of communication, reread Chapters Three and Four.

2. Written communication. Learn how to write plans and proposals effectively. (Business plans, marketing plans, investment proposals, building proposals, and the like.) Take a class if need be. Go to seminars if you must, but learn this form of communication. There are numerous books at the library on the subject of developing workable and easily understandable plans and proposals.

    Get these books and study them until you understand them and can help someone else understand them. The art of written communication is a very effective tool you must have when you are creating an atmosphere for people to be involved with your vision. Most people want to see something in writing before they will invest their time and money into a project.

The Bible encourages us to write out our vision. Habakkuk 2:2 says, "and the Lord answered me and said, write the vision, and make it plain upon tables, that he may run that readeth it." The Lord told Habakkuk to make the vision plain. This means to explain the vision in detail.

We must be able to explain the vision we have received from God on paper so when people read it they will be ready to run with it. The word *run* means to rush (7). When we explain our vision effectively on paper, there will be people who will become excited and will rush their resources to us.

3.   Oral communication. We must learn how to talk to people. Learn how to talk effectively in one-on-one conversation, group presentations, and in boardroom meetings. We have to develop strong interpersonal skills. We can read books and take communication courses so we can improve this area. We must practice, practice, and practice our public speaking so we can become better at it.

The last two areas of communication are crucial to learn. These two areas deal how you express your vision to others so they can buy in. We have to make sure that we can maneuver through these three areas so our visions can happen.

Dr. Myles Munroe said, "As a matter of fact, the purpose and goal of communication is to transfer your ideas and concept from your mind to another mind. Therefore, communication is only successful when the sender's concepts are received accurately and properly understood by the receiver and vice verse" (8).

Leadership Requirements

As you create value and credibility in your vision, others will start to look to you for leadership. As you move into your leadership role, keep at the forefront of your mind the three functions of leadership:

Mobilizing is the art of arrangement. Leaders must know how to arrange their forces. You need to know how to arrange and set up your departments. You need to have a working knowledge of how the chain of command is to flow.

You must know who's good at marketing, planning, and bookkeeping. You must be able to place people in the proper places. Leaders understand and know how to explain their business model and organizational strategy. Your business plan will lay out how your vision will operate when it is accomplished.

Energizing deals with delegation and empowerment. Leaders energize their workers when they empower them to succeed. The Apostle Paul said, "I can do all things through Christ which strengtheneth me." This is found in Philippians 4:3. This word *strengtheneth* means to empower, as defined in a previous chapter.

The apostle Paul declared to the Church at Philippi that he had the ability to do all things because Jesus Christ has empowered him. Now we do not have the capacity to empower in the same magnitude as Christ, but we can use the principle of empowerment and allow people to make decisions in their area of delegated responsibility.

People feel a sense of empowerment when they are given the authority to make a decision, and when that decision they made is carried out. Yet they must be made aware that all decisions have consequences. When we delegate responsibility to someone, we must allow him or her to have authority and the capability to make hard decisions, and to run the area or department effectively and efficiently.

You are delegating to them some of your power because you have delegated to them some of your responsibility. You must have confidence in your people to make decisions: this is how they will grow and become an instrumental part of your vision. You are communicating through your actions that you believe in your people.

Encouraging comes into play to help motivate your troops. You are encouraging them to reach toward the vision. Everyone on your team must be encouraged regularly. You encourage them by continuously sharing your vision for the future. You also encourage people when they see that you are motivated.

If you are not motivated to achieve your vision, then people will not be motivated to help you. When your people are motivated, you will move forward towards your vision. You must learn what motivates your employees, your children, your spouse, your investors, or your department heads. It is only when you understand what motivates people that you will be able to communicate effectively to influence them towards helping you reach the vision.

Moses – A Man of Leadership

Moses was a man of leadership. Let us read Exodus Chapter 18:13-26.

> And it came to pass on the morrow, that Moses sat to judge the people: and the people stood by Moses from the morning unto the evening. And when Moses' father-in-law saw all that he did to the people, he said, What is this thing that thou doest to the people? Why sittest thou thyself alone, and all the people stand by the from morning unto even: and Moses said unto his father-in-law, Because the people come unto me to enquire of God:

When they have a matter, they come unto me; and I judge between one and another, and I do make them know the statutes of God, and his laws. And Moses' father-in-law said unto him, The thing that thou doest in good. Thou wilt surely wear away, both you and this people that is with thee: for this thing is too heavy for thee: thou art not able to perform it thyself alone.

Hearken now unto my voice, I will give thee counsel, and God shall be with thee: Be thou for the people the God-ward, that thou mayest bring the cause unto God: And thou shalt teach them ordinances and laws, and shalt shew them the way wherein they must walk, and the work that thy must do. Moreover thou shalt provide out of all the people able men, such as fear God, men of truth, hating covetousness; and place such over them, to be rulers of thousands, and rulers of hundreds rulers of fifties, and rulers of tens:

And let them judge the people at all seasons: and it shall be, that every great matter they shall bring unto thee, but every small matter they shall judge: so shall it be easier for thyself, and they shall bear the burden with thee. It thou shalt do this thing, and God command thee so, then thou shalt be able to endure, and all this people shall also go to their place in peace. So Moses hearkened to the voice of his father-in-law, and did all that he had said.

And Moses chose able men out of all Israel, and made them heads over the people, rulers of thousands, rulers of hundreds, rulers of fifties, and rulers of ten. And they judged the people at all seasons: the hard causes they brought unto Moses, but every small matter they judged themselves.

In these verses, Moses is receiving counsel from his father-in-law Jethro on how to mobilize and energiz the people of Israel. Jethro is giving Moses this advice because the whole nation of Israel was coming to Moses to ask him questions on how to deal with issues in their lives.

They wanted to know what the word of God said about their problems. Jethro observed that Moses did this one activity all day long, from sun up to sun down. Jethro encouraged Moses to arrange the people of Israel into groups of tens, fifties, hundreds, and thousands. Then Jethro said to place over each group a person to handle all the matters that may arise.

If the leader over the ten could not handle the matter, the leader of the fifty would handle the issue. If he was not able to resolve the matter, it would move up to the next person in the chain of command until it reached Moses. The only way an issue would arrive before Moses was if no one in the chain of command was able to solve the problem.

Moses delegated the authority to make decisions to the individuals that were over the different groups so they could handle the problems. In another place, Moses also shared with the people of Israel a compelling vision that he received from God about their future. In Exodus 3:16-17 God told Moses:

> Go, and gather the elders of Israel together, and say unto them, the Lord God of your fathers, the God of Abraham, of Isaac, and of Jacob, appeared unto me, saying I have surely visited you and seen that which is done to you in Egypt: And I have said, I will bring you up out of the affliction of Egypt unto the land of Canaanites, and the Hittites, and the Perizzites, and the Hivites, and the Jebusites, unto a land flowing with milk and honey.

You must communicate to people your vision from God. Then you must mobilize, energize, and encourage them so the vision can be completed.

Principles

1. Leadership has three components:
   a. Mobilizing
   b. Energizing
   c. Encouraging

2. Communication is an art, not a science.

3. Being trustworthy is a result of your character and your lifestyle.

4. You must be able to express your vision to yourself and to the world.

5. Integrity is nothing more than you doing what you said you were going to do.

6. When the world sees our kingship being displayed, they should see the deeds and mannerisms of the King of Kings.

7. Good leaders know how to arrange their troops for an effective attack.

8. Learn how to influence people towards goals.

9. Learn how to delegate.

10. Encouragement must be a part of your leadership strategy if you want to reach your vision.

*

Each vision that is actualized is a part of your purpose being manifested.

You have to manage and control an obtained vision for future growth.

*

Chapter Six:
Actualization of the Vision

I have glorified thee on the earth: I have finished the work which thou gavest me to do.
-John 17:4-

Within this chapter we will deal with your vision being achieved. It is important for us to persevere until the end. To fight on until all has been accomplished.

You must remember that God gave you the vision and you have been impregnated with possibilities. Be encouraged; if you do not quit, your vision will manifest. If you don't give up, you will reap the fulfillment of your purpose and actualize your leadership.

The Principle of Stewardship

During the process of manifesting the vision, you must understand the principle of stewardship. Being a good steward over the vision that God has given you is the prerequisite for moving to the next level and receiving another revelation. Stewardship is management.

To be a great manager, you must be a great steward. Jesus expressed this concept of stewardship and servitude in Mark 13:34. "For the Son of man is as a man taking a far journey, who left his house, and gave authority to his servants, and to every man his work, and commanded the porter to watch."

Here are some observations about this passage of scripture. The first observation is that a man left his servants with authority. The word *authority* means ability, privilege, freedom, mastery, and delegated influence (1). These words describe perfectly our restored roles of leadership. God has given to blood-washed believers delegated influence.

He has given to us the power to influence the affairs that are occurring on earth. He has giving us the ability and privilege to represent Him as ambassadors of the kingdom of Glory here on earth. He has given us the freedom to master and handle our situations and circumstances through the power of the Holy Spirit.

This man left his servants with authority over his house. They were to govern the affairs of their master while he was away. The visions God will give you will be the affairs He wants you to handle while Jesus is away in heaven. God has given us the authority to manage our visions.

Rich Marshall, the author of *God@Work* writes, "When God's authority resides in you, there is no backing down. Divine authority brings with it a boldness that cannot be diminished or turned aside" (2).

Marshall also declares, "Since this authority is God – given, it is not limited to those we would delegate it to based on human reasoning. One of the most noticeable and truest sign for marketplace transformation is authority" (3). The master's affairs must be accomplished while He is in glory ruling on His throne.

Another observation about Mark 13:34 is that every man (and woman) had work to do. The master left everyone with a job to complete. Understand that every one of God's children has a purpose to manifest. Everyone has a vision to fulfill. Everyone has a job and a destiny. Everyone has a God-given goal to accomplish.

Managing the Vision

Now, once the vision is here you must oversee it. You have to watch it and take care of it like a growing baby. God gave this vision to you, so it is your responsibility to manage it. Understand that with every blessing comes responsibility.

Winston Churchill said it perfectly: "The price of greatness is responsibility." Just because a person has the ability to be a visionary, that does not qualify them to be a manager. They are different functions within an organization; while a person can do both functions, that does not make the functions identical.

A visionary can be seen as the architect of the vision. This is the person who puts the vision on paper (blueprint). The manager can be compared to a general contractor. This individual is the one who make sure that the workers follow the blueprint (vision). Let us compare the two:

Visionary and Manager Comparison

Let us compare three characteristics to find out how a visionary differs from a manager.

I.
The Visionary:
Focus on direction – The visionary declares to the organization 'this is the way we are headed'. The visionary paints a picture of the final destination.

The Manager:
Focus on organizing – The manager's function is to organize the troops and resources to carry out the mission of going towards the final destination.

II.
The Visionary:
Doing the right things – The visionary's focus is external, and makes sure that the company is in the right industry based on the enterprise's competencies, workforce, and resources.

The Manager:
Doing things right – The manager's focus is internal, making sure that within the company they have the proper systems, procedures, and protocols based on industry standards.

III.
The Visionary:

Working on the vision – Visionaries continually fine-tune the picture that has been revealed to them. They work on communicating it effectively and constantly keeping it before the people.

The Manager:

Working within the vision – The manager concentrates on the interior components of the business, such as working with the employees who are working the systems and following the procedures and protocol.

Always remember, God has given you authority over your vision to run it, control it, and govern it for his glory. Do not allow people to take control of your vision and run it the way they want to. God gave you that vision, not them.

Stand up for yourself. Stand up and lead with the authority God has given you. You have to learn how to manage your vision from God. You must oversee the vision as a person of integrity for the glory of the King.

Management Development

Managing your vision requires you to learn the skills of management. Great managers are not born with excellent management talents. They became that way through learning, training and experience.

To be an effective manager, you must learn the skills necessary to grow a business, family, or church fellowship. It does not matter the vision or the entity, we must learn to be good stewards. When a person is in a leadership role, that does not mean they will be an effective manager.

As declared above, visionaries and managers focus on different activities. A visionary usually falls under the function of leadership. Leadership concentrates on leading, energizing, empowering, and inspiring people. Managers focus on managing things such as profit, cash flow, procedures, and systems.

Let us look at two components of effective management.

1. Money Matters
2. Best Practices

While this section will talk about these two components from a business perspective, they can also be abled to family matters. The first point we will talk about is money. Money is a crucial part of running an organization and making it grow. Understanding how money works, specifically cash flow and profit, will solidify the operation of your vision. Cash flow is the food for your vision.

As the human body needs food to live, a vision must have cash flow to prosper and thrive in the world. To get a grip on cash flow you must understand how money flows in and out of your organization. You must find out how much your venture is bringing in daily, weekly, monthly, and annually through the sales of your products and services.

The cash flow and the profitability of your organization will determine if you will be able to continually invest in the vision to make it grow. Having your business operate at a healthy profit margin will attract more money to your vision through grants, angel investors, venture capitalists, and tax incentives.

As a leader of an organization, you have to know how to read numbers. You read the numbers by being able to read financial statements. You must learn how to read financial statements, balance sheet, and income statements. The way you read financial statements are through financial formulas. The formulas will help you understand how your organization is doing.

When you use the formulas, you will be able to take the numbers and compare them to the industry standards. This way you can find out if your organization is measuring up to other businesses in your field. There are books and publications available that will tell you the financial standards for just about any industry.

For example, let's talk about profit. What is profit? It is the leftover money from the sale of your product after you have paid your bills. A simple formula for profit is: income – expenses = profit.

You would get those numbers from your financial statements. By plugging the numbers into the formula and doing the math, you will get your answer. To be a good steward, you must focus on having healthy profit margins and consistent cash flow. Many good books have been written to show you which formulas to use and how to use them.

Not only do you need to think about financial matters, you will also want to think about best practices. What are best practices? They are the current best way to do a task. You want to search for the best practices for your vision.

You need to ask yourself and others, "What are the best ways of doing tasks within this industry, and in particularly in this business?" While some best practices cross over multiple industries, others are specific to the organization you are building. You want to learn them and see if they will fit into your organization.

You will want to document the best practices that you will use in our business within your organization's Standard Operating Procedures (SOP). Your SOP will be the way you, and those who work with you, will operate the organization. Using the SOP will help your organization become systems (process) dependent instead of personality-dependent.

To find out the best practices for your industry, you must do your research. You want to look at the best companies in your industry, and if possible in the world. You want find out how those organizations operate.

If there is an organization like your vision, go there and take notes. Look at everything you can. Look at their processes; see how they treat their customers and their employees. You have to become curious and attempt to learn all you can about your future organization.

The name of the game is research, research, and more research.

Another name for a practice is a *system*. Systems creation will help your business or nonprofit organization run more effectively and be more innovative.

Systems creation

Systems creation is how managers develop their organizations. A system is an organized process that produces the same outcome every single time. It is the ability to perform an action the same way every time. Your organization must be systems-dependent and not personality-reliant.

Systems are the components that bridge the gap for organizations that desire to cross from the wilderness of chaos into the plush pastures of effective organization. Enterprises that are effective and efficient are built on solid functioning systems. If you want to know how sound an organization is, examine their systems.

Building systems or practices into your business will help it grow and become all that God has ordained it to be. You must examine every component of your vision and break it down into specific practices, and then document them in your SOP.

When you are designing your systems, focus on making them effective and performance-based. Who determines if your systems are effective and functional? Your customers do. You are creating systems so your vision can run like a well-oiled machine, so that when your customers come to patronize your organization you are satisfying their needs.

God's marketing system

God put a system in place when he decided to send Jesus to earth and proclaim that the Kingdom of God had arrived. Then he had the system documented in his SOP, the Bible. God used a systemic word-of-mouth approach to communicate the Gospel of the Kingdom, which is effective marketing at its best. Let us see how God marketed the Kingdom of Heaven.

The Bible says the first person that came on the scene proclaiming the kingdom's message was John the Baptist. The Baptist appeared in the wilderness of Judea declaring, "Repent ye: for the kingdom of heaven is at hand" (Matt. 3:2). Then King Jesus appeared and proclaimed, "Repent: for the kingdom of heaven is at hand" (Matt. 4:17).

Next, when Jesus sent out the twelve disciples to preach he told them, "And as ye go, preach, saying, The kingdom of heaven is at hand" (Matt. 10:7). We see in the book of Luke where Jesus appointed seventy disciples and sent them out in twos to preach. He told them to tell the people "The kingdom of God is come nigh unto you" (Luke 10:9).

Can you see how God orchestrated the words to proclaim that the kingdom of God had arrived on earth? God systemically announced the arrival of the kingdom of heaven.

Diamond Formula

One way to have an effective organization is to use the Diamond Formula. The Diamond Formula is a methodology that is used to create functional systems. It is a systematic approach to creating effective systems and practices.

The formula has *diamond* as its name, because a diamond is known to be the hardest natural material. Using the Diamond Formula will turn your vision into a solid, thriving enterprise. This methodology has four stages and they are:

A. Inception – Target stage
B. Experimentation – Pilot stage
C. Standardization – Solidify stage

    D. Incorporation – Elevation stage
    Let us take a brief look at each stage.

Inception

Inception starts with the ideal function of a system. Within this stage, you identify the reason for the system. Then you clearly explain why you need the system. After you have explained the reason why you need it, you must brainstorm to come up with different ways of getting the customer experience you want.

When that is completed, you must plan out the experimental process with objectives and specific goals. The last component of this stage is determining how much the system is going to cost, if it is worth the risk, and what the benefits are.

Experimentation

In the experimentation stage, you try out (pilot) your new system. As you are piloting your system, make sure you do not test more than one at a time. The reason for this is that during this stage you are tracking and measuring the system to find out if it meets the objectives and goals that you have planned for it.

The experimentation stage is where you test the system to see if it will fail. This is when you determine if the system works and if it needs to be optimized, refined, or thrown away. During the pilot stage there are no "sacred cows". If it does not work, toss it.

Standardization

The standardization stage is where you document how to perform the system. During this stage, you are creating your standards of excellence (processes). Standardization is when you write down your "recipe" to produce your desired outcome. When you are solidifying your system, make sure you are working with the end in mind.

Start with how the process is to look and perform. Then write down the items or ingredients needed to perform the process. Finally, document the steps that must be taken to perform the system so it appears the way it is supposed to look. The goal of this stage is to make the system functional and repeatable.

Incorporation

The incorporation stage is when you elevate your new system company-wide. This is when you roll out the process for everyone in the enterprise to learn and work. You are integrating this new system into your operating model. Your operating model is the manifestation of your Standard Operating Procedures.

The beginning portion of the elevation is training. Do not, and I repeat do not, hand out your manuals and expect for your followers to simply perform the new process. You must train the people within your organization. The final step is continuous improvement, where you are continually monitoring, tracking, and managing your system.

Principles

1. As long as you stay focused on Christ's directions, you will accomplish the vision God has given you.

2. After your vision has been obtained, it has to be managed.

3. A visionary is the architect that creates the blueprint of the future.

4. A manager can be compared to a general contractor, who makes sure the workers are working toward manifesting the blueprint.

5. God has given you authority over your vision to run it, control it, and govern it for his glory.

6. Great managers are not born with excellent management skills -- they develop them.

7. Two components of effective management:
   A. Money Matters
   B. Best Practices

8. Your organization must have Standard Operating Procedures.

9. Businesses that are successful enterprises are built on solid functioning systems.

10. The Diamond Formula has four components:
    A. Inception – Target stage
    B. Experimentation – Pilot stage
    C. Standardization – Solidify stage
    D. Incorporation – Elevation stage

The Conclusion

*Then I saw a new heaven and a new earth, for the old
heaven and the old earth had disappeared.
-Revelation 21:1-*

Let us go over what we have examined thus far:

1. A revealed vision from God.
2. An uncovered purpose by God.
3. Our thinking must be renewed.
4. Actions bring the vision to life.
5. The art of communication is very important.

Revealed Vision

Your vision must come from God. He must be the
originator of your dreams. For your vision to stand the
test of time, it must be a revelation from the Almighty
King of Eternity. Whatever God has shown you, reach
for it and do not quit until it is completed. It does not
matter what the vision is, whether it be a missionary
crusade, building a worship center, starting a business
venture, having a solid Christian family, or getting
your college degree.

We must remember to connect our goals to our
vision to help us in the direction toward manifestation.
Your vision will always have something to do with
exalting the King of Glory on Earth. When God

reveals the vision to you, it will begin to establish you and begin to make apparent your leadership through Christ Jesus.

"Where there is no vision, the people perish"
(Prov. 29:18)

An Uncovered Purpose

Our visions are revealed to us, therefore our purpose in life must also be revealed to us. Remember that your purpose is connected to your vision. Portions of your purpose are exposed to you when your vision is revealed to you. Then as your vision is actualized, a part of your purpose for being alive is manifested.

Your purpose is your *why*. It is the reason behind your existence. It is why God created you. Your purpose is God's will for your life.

If God does not reveal to you his will for your life, you will never know who you truly are. A creation will never know its reason for being made unless the Creator exposes the creature to it. As you are manifesting your purpose for being alive, others will see your role as being a leader on this earth.

And that servant, which knew his lord's will, and prepared not himself, neither did according to his will, shall be beaten with many stripes. But he that knew not, and did commit things worthy of stripes, shall be beaten with few stripes. For unto whomsoever much is given, of

154

him shall be much required: and to whom men have committed much, of him they will ask the more. (Luke 12:47-48)

Renewed Thinking

Our minds must be renewed so we can reach our vision and manifest our purpose. This is why we must have a prayerful spirit. Negative thoughts must be pruned and replaced with the Word of God.

We must have our Ideals changed to possibility thinking. Start seeing the possibilities God has created for you because you are his child. Your thinking has to change so you can pursue with all your might God's will for your life.

That ye put off concerning the former conversation the old man, which is corrupt according to the deceitful lusts; and be renewed in the spirit of your mind; and that ye put on the new man, which after God is created in righteousness and true holiness. (Eph. 4:22-24)

Actions of Manifestation

Without **action** nothing will get done! Without action your vision will not be achieved. You must work hard at getting your vision accomplished. It will not be easy, but it will be worth it.

You have to get involved in making your vision come to pass. You have to find actions that will help you succeed in life. Then you will turn those actions into habits.

Then we must find other actions that we can turn into habits and do this process repeatedly. We will do this until we have an arsenal of positive habitual actions pushing us forward to our position of leadership. Action is a major key, which opens the door to your vision and the manifestation of your purpose.

> And the recompense of a man's hands shall be
> rendered unto him.
> (Prov. 12:14)

The Art of Communication

Learning the art of communication is essential. Talking to people is an art, not a science. A conversation has to flow and be creative.

You must know how to communicate intelligently your vision for the future. You must learn how to talk to people. You have to increase your interpersonal skills.

We need to focus on the three areas of communication.

1. Internal communication
2. Written communication
3. Oral communication

We must be able to use these three aspects of communication easily and on a regular basis so others can buy into our visions. As our leadership grows, we must keep in mind the three areas of leadership:

1. Mobilization
2. Energizing
3. Inspiration

> And the Lord answered me, and said, Write the vision, and make it plain upon tables, that he may run that readeth it. For the vision is yet for an appointed time, but at the end it shall speak, and not lie: though it tarry, wait for it; because it will surely come, it will not tarry. (Hab. 2:2-3)

Actualization of the vision

This is where we learned how to manage the vision that God has given to us. In this section we also learned that being a good steward was foundational to being an effective manager. From this chapter we compared the differences between visionaries and managers.

Because a person has a vision, that does not mean he or she has an innate ability to run the vision properly. To become a good manager, you must learn the skills of effective management. A competent manager understands that money matters and knows the best practices of the industry.

Finally, we were exposed to the Diamond Formula.

This methodology has four components:

A. Inception – Target stage
B. Experimentation – Pilot stage
C. Standardization – Solidify stage
D. Incorporation – Elevation stage

I have glorified thee on the earth: I have finished the work which thou gavest me to do.
(John 17:4)

In conclusion, we have the awesome responsibility of reaching out and helping the brethren. Your vision is not only about your leadership. God's plan is bigger than one person. God's desire is that all of his children mature to the fullness and stature of his son Jesus, our Lord and Savior.

Spiritual Mentors

It is important that we become mentors and reach out to encourage our brothers and sisters in Christ as they pursue their vision from God. The concept of mentoring can be found within scripture.

Moses mentored Joshua. Elijah mentored Elisha. Jesus mentored the twelve apostles. We must become mentors by following the steps of our Biblical heritage.

The Apostle Paul was a mentor. He mentored Timothy, the Bishop of Ephesus. Timothy was raised in a bicultural home -- his father was Greek and his mother was a Jewish Christian (Acts 16:1). Paul took Timothy under his wing and started training him under the power of the Holy Spirit on how to be a leader.

Timothy went on missionary journeys with Paul and learned how to preach and teach about Jesus Christ and the Kingdom of God (Acts 17:13-15). Timothy was there when Paul wrote some of his epistles to churches (Phil. 1:1). When Timothy became Bishop of Ephesus, Paul encouraged him on how to run the church (1, 2 Tim.).

Paul and Timothy had such a good relationship that the Apostle refers to Timothy as his "son in the faith" (I Tim. 1:2). Paul trained Timothy on how to be a true man of God and a humble servant to God's people. That is the importance of mentoring: we, working with the Holy Spirit, mold people into the individuals God has ordained them to be. Kenneth Blanchard and Spencer Johnson write, "The Best Minute I spend is the one I invest in people" (1).

As we go through the process of being good stewards, we will show others how to live out their purpose and accomplish their visions. When we are being good stewards, we can say and display with confidence what the Apostle Paul said to the church in

Corinth, "Be ye followers of me, even as I also am of Christ" (1 Cor. 11:1).

Paul was telling the Christians at Corinth to follow his example. He was providing an example of how to live for the glory of God. He told them to follow him by living their lives for God. The apostle Paul was telling them to imitate his life and actions.

You will have the ability to declare the same information with other believers as you seek after the Lord. As you strive to reach your destiny, you will be an example to others that they can also fulfill their roles of leadership.

Our lives will show them they can do it and achieve their vision. A foundational practice within Christianity is being an example to others on how to live for God. In the second book to the Thessalonians, the Apostle Paul said he and the other Apostles were an example for the church of Jesus Christ.

Modeling

The last portion of 2 Thessalonians 3:9 says, "to make ourselves an enample unto you to follow us." An *ensample* means to model for imitation (5). We must employ the concept of modeling. Modeling is not about putting on a show or an act for people to see you perform and say how great you are. It is the practice of being an example for others, to help them be all they can be for the glory of God. Stephen R. Covey wrote,

"Modeling is the spirit and center of any leadership effort" (2).

We can be the example others will look to when they need to see people who have accomplished their visions. We can be the people they remember when times get hard and they want to quit. You must understand, your arriving at your destiny is not only about you. It's also about helping others to reach their visions so they will be able to live a victorious life too.

It is of the utmost importance that we reach out and help someone reach his or her God-given vision. Encouraging others is a part of everyone's vision and purpose. You must help people grow and develop into who they were created to be.

This will help us leave a legacy on earth when we die. We are to leave something behind that will stand the duration of time. We do that by influencing people to follow their God-given visions.

Legacy building

A legacy is not about making a name for yourself or esteeming yourself higher than you ought. It is about doing something that will last and endure for generations, to use and to be inspired. That is exactly what Jesus did.

Jesus created a legacy called Christianity. A legacy is something that is passed down from one generation to the next generation. It started with Jesus, and then it moved to the Apostles.

Then it moved to the one hundred and twenty people who were in the upper room in Jerusalem. Then it spread to the three thousand people who were saved on the day of Pentecost through the preaching of the Apostle Peter. After that, Christianity invaded the world and transformed it.

That is the power of doing the will of God. It can transform the world. Jesus modeled to his disciples how to live. He is our model. He should be the Ideal person we think about when it comes to being a visionary and a legacy builder.

We must follow Christ and be visionaries and people of purpose. Generations to come are looking to us for support and encouragement on how to live for the glory of God. Future Christ followers need to see people seeking God for visions and purpose.

The world is counting on you. Your community is counting on you. Your family is counting on you. Your God is counting on you to obey his will and to achieve your vision.

You can do it. You can create a legacy and manifest your purpose. Walter Lippman declared, "The final test of a leader is that he leaves behind him in other men the conviction and the will to carry on" (3). You can achieve your vision from God.

Go for it -- you cannot lose. God is on your side. If God be for you, he is more than the whole world against you. Mark Hopkins writes, "Certainly no revolution that has ever taken place in society can be compared to that which has been produced by the words of Jesus Christ" (4).

It is your turn to participate in the revolution. You are now required to take your rightful position of leadership. Today is the day for you to seek God for your revelation so you can pursue your purpose and become the revolutionary leader you are destined to be.

I leave you with the word of Dr. Myles Munroe, "When God created mankind to have dominion over the earth, He imparted to us ability to govern, rule, lead, and manage the earth, its creatures, and resources. We are designed to rule, not be ruled. We are designed to govern, not be governed. We are designed to manage, not be managed. We are designed to lead, not to follow" (5).

Works Cited

Introduction:

1. Andrews, Robert. <u>The Concise Columbia</u>
   <u>Dictionary of Quotation</u>.
   >Benjamin Disraeli (1804-1881)
   >Columbia University Press. New York.
   >P. 227
2. Hamon, Dr. Bill. <u>The Day of the Saints</u>.
   Destiny Publisher, Inc.
   >p. 211

Chapter One:

1. Strong, James. <u>The New Strong's Exhaustive</u>
   <u>Concordance of the</u>
   <u>Bible</u>. Thomas Nelson Publishers. p.1417
   definition # 2377
2. Strong, James. <u>The New Strong's Exhaustive</u>
   <u>Concordance of the</u>
   <u>Bible</u>. Thomas Nelson Publishers. p.1028
   definition # 6544
3. Strong, James. <u>The New Strong's Exhaustive</u>
   <u>Concordance of the</u>
   <u>Bible</u>. Thomas Nelson Publishers. p.1235
   definition # 4591
4. Strong, James. <u>The New Strong's Exhaustive</u>
   <u>Concordance of the</u>
   <u>Bible</u>. Thomas Nelson Publishers. p.1216
   definition # 312

5. Strong, James. The New Strong's Exhaustive Concordance of the Bible. Thomas Nelson Publishers. p.759 definition # 1492
6. Strong, James. The New Strong's Exhaustive Concordance of the Bible. Thomas Nelson Publishers. p.1421 definition # 5456
7. Nee, Watchman. The Spiritual Man. Volume II. Christian Fellowship Publisher, Inc. p. 71
8. Evans, Tony. The Kingdom Agenda. Moody Publishers. Chicago, IL

9. Strong, James. The New Strong's Exhaustive Concordance of the Bible. Thomas Nelson Publishers. p.1026 definition # 1921
10. Covey, Stephen R. The 8th Habit. Free Press. New York. P. 157

Chapter Two:

1. Schuller, Robert H. Self Esteem The New Reformation. Word Books Publisher Waco, Texas. P. 33-34.
2. Murdock, Mike. 101 Wisdom Keys. The Wisdom Center. Denton Texas. P. 16
3. Warren, Rick. Purpose Driven Church. ZONERVAN. Grand Rapids, Michigan p. 87

4. Blackaby, Henry. <u>Chosen to be God's Prophet</u>. Thomas Nelson Publishers. Nashville, Tennessee. P. 133

5. Strong, James. <u>The New Strong's Exhaustive Concordance of the Bible</u>. Thomas Nelson Publishers. p.1319 definition # 3533

6. Strong, James. <u>The New Strong's Exhaustive Concordance of the Bible</u>. Thomas Nelson Publishers. p.322 definition # 7281

7. Munroe, Myles. <u>Rediscovering the Kingdom</u>. Destiny Image Publishers. Shippensburg, PA. p. 35

8. Munroe, Myles. <u>Rediscovering the Kingdom</u>. Destiny Image Publishers. Shippensburg, PA. p. 21

9. Strong, James. <u>The New Strong's Exhaustive Concordance of the Bible</u>. Thomas Nelson Publishers. p.755 definition # 3045

10. Covey, Stephen R. <u>The 8th Habit</u>. Free Press. New York. P. 28

Chapter Three:

1. Strong, James. <u>The New Strong's Exhaustive Concordance of the Bible.</u> Thomas Nelson Publishers. p.1352 definition # 8176

2. Strong, James. <u>The New Strong's Exhaustive Concordance of the</u>

Bible. Thomas Nelson Publishers. p.588
definition # 5315

3. Strong, James. The New Strong's Exhaustive Concordance of the Bible. Thomas Nelson Publishers. p.588 definition # 3820

4. Anderson, Neil T, Zuehlke, Terry E, Zuehlke, Julianne S. Christ Centered Therapy. Zondervan Publishing House. Grand Rapids, Michigan. P. 106

5. Strong, James. The New Strong's Exhaustive Concordance of the Bible. Thomas Nelson Publishers. p.232 definition # 2974

6. Simcox, Carroll E. A Treasury of Quotations on Christian Themes. Anonymous. p. 158

7. Simcox, Carroll E. A Treasury of Quotations on Christian Themes. Raven, Charles E. p. 158

8. Anderson, Neil T, Zuehlke, Terry E, Zuehlke, Julianne S. Christ Centered Therapy. Zondervan Publishing House. Grand Rapids, Michigan. P. 105

9. Strong, James. The New Strong's Exhaustive Concordance of the Bible. Thomas Nelson Publishers. p.1120 definition # 365

10. Munroe, Myles. Rediscovering the Kingdom. Destiny Image Publishers. Shippensburg, PA. p. 59

11. Strong, James. <u>The New Strong's Exhaustive Concordance of the Bible</u>. Thomas Nelson Publishers. p.1291 definition # 4151
12. Strong, James. <u>The New Strong's Exhaustive Concordance of the Bible</u>. Thomas Nelson Publishers. p.376 definition # 7592
13. Strong, James. <u>The New Strong's Exhaustive Concordance of the Bible</u>. Thomas Nelson Publishers. p.1314 definition # 1743

Chapter Four:

1. Robbins, Anthony, McClendon, Joseph III. <u>Unlimited Power – A Black Choice</u>. Simon & Schuster. New York. p. 44
2. Strong, James. <u>The New Strong's Exhaustive Concordance of the Bible</u>. Thomas Nelson Publishers. p.1316 definition # 75
3. Strong, James. <u>The New Strong's Exhaustive Concordance of the Bible</u>. Thomas Nelson Publishers. p.1341 definition # 1467
4. Strong, James. <u>The New Strong's Exhaustive Concordance of the Bible</u>. Thomas Nelson Publishers. p.729 definition # 5299
5. Robbins, Anthony, McClendon, Joseph III. <u>Unlimited Power – A</u>

Black Choice. Simon & Schuster. New York. p. 44

6. Strong, James. The New Strong's Exhaustive Concordance of the Bible. Thomas Nelson Publishers. p.322 definition # 4163

7. Strong, James. The New Strong's Exhaustive Concordance of the Bible. Thomas Nelson Publishers. p.288 definition # 3884

8. Covey, Stephen R. The 8th Habit. Free Press. New York.

9. Simcox, Carroll E. A Treasury of Quotations on Christian Themes. Dryden, John. p. 85

10. Simcox, Carroll E. A Treasury of Quotations on Christian Themes. Pascal, Blaise. p. 85

Chapter Five:

1. Covey, Stephen R. The 8th Habit. Free Press. New York. P. 157

2. Strong, James. The New Strong's Exhaustive Concordance of the Bible. Thomas Nelson Publishers. p.1387 definition # 982

3. Lee, Blaine. The Power Principle. Simon & Schuster. New York. p. 166

4. Simcox, Carroll E. A Treasury of Quotations on Christian Themes. Washington, George. p. 179

5.   Strong, James. <u>The New Strong's Exhaustive</u>
     <u>Concordance of the</u>
     <u>Bible</u>. Thomas Nelson Publishers. p.459
     definition # 3402
6.   Drucker, Peter F. <u>The Effective Execute</u>.
     Harper & Row Publishers.
     New York. p. 23
7.   Munroe, Myles. <u>Rediscovering the Kingdom</u>.
     Destiny Image
     Publishers. Shippensburg, PA. p. 59

Chapter Six:

1.   Strong, James. <u>The New Strong's Exhaustive</u>
     <u>Concordance of the</u>
     <u>Bible</u>. . Thomas Nelson Publishers. p.63
     definition # 1849
2.   Marshall, Rich. <u>God@Work Volume 2</u>.
     Destiny Image Publishers,
     Inc. Shippensburg, PA. p. 64
3.   Marshall, Rich. <u>God@Work Volume 2</u>.
     Destiny Image Publishers,
     Inc. Shippensburg, PA. p. 65

Conclusion

1.   Blanchard, Kenneth, Johnson, Spencer. <u>The</u>
     <u>One Minute Manager</u>.
     Berkley Books. New York. p. 63
2.   Covey, Stephen R. <u>The 8th Habit</u>. Free Press.
     New York.

3. Simcox, Carroll E. <u>A Treasury of Quotations on Christian Themes</u>.
   Lippman, Walter. p. 93
4. Simcox, Carroll E. <u>A Treasury of Quotations on Christian Themes</u>.
   Hopkins, Mark. p.105
5. Munroe, Myles. <u>Rediscovering the Kingdom</u>.
   Destiny Image
   Publishers. Shippensburg, PA.

Stephen Owens is a pastor, church planter and writer. He is the pastor at Mt. Calvary Baptist Church in Bedford, Ohio. Before becoming the pastor of Mt. Calvary Stephen planted Triumphant Assembly - A CHURCH FOR THOSE THAT WANT MORE OUT OF LIFE. Stephen has over 18 years of ministry experience, which ranges from Sunday school teacher to pastor. Stephen has a passion for encouraging leaders to be all that God wants them to be. Whether they are in the marketplace or in the church Stephen has an encouraging word for them.

How to contact Stephen:

Email: Stephen_owens_ministries@yahoo.com

Website: www.mtcalvaryofbedford.org

Facebook:
https://www.facebook.com/DevelopingLeadership

Twitter: @Owens_Ministry

Stephen is available for the following events:
1. Conferences
2. Preaching Engagements
3. Workshops
4. Book Signings

Listen to Stephen's sermon series:
www.mtcalvaryofbedford.org/media

www.ingramcontent.com/pod-product-compliance
Lightning Source LLC
Chambersburg PA
CBHW021828020426
42334CB00014B/541